Who Will Fight the Next War?

Martin Binkin

Who Will Fight the Next War?

The Changing Face of the American Military

The Brookings Institution
Washington, D.C.

Copyright © 1993 by
THE BROOKINGS INSTITUTION
1775 Massachusetts Avenue, N.W., Washington, D.C. 20036

Library of Congress Cataloging-in-Publication Data:

Binkin, Martin, 1928–
   Who will fight the next war?   :   the changing face of the American military /
Martin Binkin.
      p.   cm.
   Includes bibliographical references and index.
   ISBN 0-8157-0956-0—ISBN 0-8157-0955-2
   1. United States—Armed Forces—Reorganization. I. Title.
UA23.B498   1993
355'.00973'09049—dc20   93-9981
                                                                              CIP

9 8 7 6 5 4 3 2 1

The paper used in this publication meets the minimum requirements of the
American National Standard for Information Sciences—Permanence of Paper for
Printed Library Materials, ANSI Z39.48—1984.

Foreword

WHEN the United States ended conscription two decades ago, it embarked on a bold and unprecedented experiment: raising superpower-size military forces by strictly voluntary means. After a difficult period of transition in the 1970s, the armed forces have now attracted the best educated and most trainable recruits in history. The forces have also experienced dramatic changes in composition as record numbers of African Americans and women have enlisted and reserves have become more important to the nation's military plans.

Martin Binkin has been a close observer of these changes. In a series of Brookings studies he has warned that, although these trends reflect the nation's earnest efforts to achieve equal opportunity and to strengthen the link between the armed forces and society, they could lead to troublesome social and political problems in wartime that might compromise military effectiveness.

In *Women and the Military* (1977) Binkin and his coauthor criticized the Pentagon's failure to assign women to fill a wide range of noncombat jobs and encouraged the services to initiate a test program to gather data on the performance of women in combat units. *Blacks and the Military* (1982) brought attention to the dramatic growth in the participation of blacks in the all-volunteer force. It cautioned that the benefits they received from disproportionate representation in peacetime needed to be considered against the possibility of disproportionate casualties in wartime. *U.S. Army Guard and Reserve* (1988) concluded that the army was relying excessively on its reserve components and warned that the capabilities of the army national guard combat units were being overstated.

In *Who Will Fight the Next War?* the author revisits these issues in light of the Persian Gulf conflict, the first major combat test for the all-volunteer force. He analyzes the roles of women, African Americans, and citizen-soldiers in the military and provides options that should be considered in decisions about the composition of America's armed forces in the post–cold war world.

The author thanks Carolyn Becraft, Mark Eitelberg, Beth Flores, Bernard Rostker, Carol Schuster, and Neil Singer for their comments on the manuscript. He is also indebted to Brookings colleagues Thomas Berry, Joe Crookston, MacArthur DeShazer, Edwin Dorn, Thom Ford, and Lawrence Korb for their critiques of the manuscript and is grateful to John D. Steinbruner, director of the Brookings Foreign Policy Studies program, who provided valuable guidance. The staff of the Defense Manpower Data Center and especially Zietta Ferris were very helpful in providing data.

James Schneider edited the manuscript, Adrianne Goins and Myles Nienstadt verified its factual content, Ann Ziegler processed it, and Max Franke compiled the index.

The institution gratefully acknowledges the assistance of the Ford Foundation, whose grant helped to support this study.

The views expressed here are those of the author and should not be ascribed to the persons who provided data or commented on the manuscript, the Ford Foundation, or the trustees, officers, or other staff members of the Brookings Institution.

BRUCE K. MAC LAURY
President

May 1993
Washington, D.C.

Contents

Tables

Figures

CHAPTER ONE

The Changing Face of the Military

IN THE TWO DECADES since the end of conscription, the United States has fashioned a military of unparalleled diversity. Once staffed almost exclusively by men, in racial proportions roughly mirroring the American population, and dependent on reserves and the National Guard only in the most extreme emergency, the contemporary armed forces are now made up of unprecedented proportions of women and blacks and rely more than ever before on their reserve components.

The all-volunteer era has seen women make strong inroads into many military assignments that were once exclusively male preserves. Since 1970, the proportion of women in the armed forces has grown from less than 2 percent to more than 11 percent, and the proportion assigned to the traditionally female health care and clerical jobs has plummeted from more than 90 percent to less than 50 percent.

African Americans, facing relatively dim employment prospects in the 1970s and 1980s, also joined the new volunteer military in record numbers. Their proportion in the armed forces grew from 10 percent in the early 1970s to 20 percent by the beginning of the 1990s. The growth was especially noticeable in the Army, where they increased from about 14 percent to 30 percent of the enlisted ranks in these years.

The nation's citizen-soldiers, too, were beneficiaries of the decision to abandon conscription. Under a new "total force" policy, the reserve forces became the primary means of expanding U.S. military capabilities in an emergency. This change ushered in a renaissance for the weekend warriors. Equipment was upgraded, training improved, and reserve participation in supporting the nation's security became increasingly prom-

1

inent. Under the Army's cold war contingency plans, for example, reserve units were to be among the earliest deployed and were to provide the bulk of support troops in everything from fast-breaking limited conflicts to a major confrontation in central Europe between NATO and the Warsaw Pact.

This changing face of the American military, dictated by the end of the draft and various economic, social, and political forces, was hailed for reflecting the nation's equal opportunity goals, strengthening the link, weakened by the Vietnam experience, between the military and society, and producing the most able American military force since World War II.

But the military had not been tested in major combat, and skeptics were concerned that the changes might compromise the effectiveness and efficiency of wartime operations by raising troublesome political and social concerns. Black Americans benefited from participation in the peacetime military, for example, but would they suffer disproportionate casualties in wartime? The more varied military assignments for women represented a success in their achieving equal opportunity but left hanging the question of how their presence would affect military efficiency in wartime. And the wider and earlier reliance on reserve forces, according to critics, had been based as much on political as on military considerations, raising doubts that the forces were as prepared and potentially effective as total force pronouncements implied.

As long as the nation was at peace, these matters were left to academics to discuss. But when Iraq occupied Kuwait in August 1990, the prospect that America's volunteer force would soon be involved in a major ground war aroused considerable public interest, widespread debate, and a good deal of worry.

Many African American leaders, some of whom had applauded the growing participation of blacks in the peacetime military, now feared that blacks would bear more than a fair share of the casualties. The deployment of record numbers of military women to a combat theater was greeted with public ambivalence as many people realized, seemingly for the first time, that equal opportunity might well mean equal peril. And despite the rhetoric that had accompanied the total force policy, the readiness and capabilities of the reserve forces came under serious question.

Fortunately, with the quick end to the conflict, these matters failed to develop into real problems. Had the Gulf action been as protracted and as bloody as many experts expected, concerns about casualties among blacks and women would have deepened rapidly, eroding public support for what most Americans believed was a just war and intensifying racial and social divisions in American society. And given the unpreparedness of the Army combat reserves, the Pentagon would probably have discovered that it had overestimated the nation's military capabilities.

It is important that questions involving the composition of the armed forces be resolved so that they will not haunt future military conflicts. Settling them, however, will be no mean task. The peacetime benefit–wartime burden that blacks experience poses a difficult dilemma for American society. And what duties can be assigned to women in the military puts two powerful imperatives—national security and equal opportunity—on a collision course. Finally, devising an appropriate role for the nation's reserves will require neutralizing the politics—both legislative and bureaucratic—that traditionally have shaped the size and use of these forces.

This study does not seek to settle these questions. Its purpose is more modest: to contribute to a better understanding of the issues. Chapter 2 traces the evolution of the use of women in the nation's armed forces, focusing on the expansion in their numbers and duties that accompanied the end of conscription. It examines how they fared in the Persian Gulf conflict and the implications of their performance for their future roles, especially in combat. Chapter 3 analyzes the benefits versus burdens dilemma that underlies the question of the appropriate extent of participation by blacks in the nation's armed services. It discusses the factors that have contributed to the strong propensity of African Americans for military service, their experience in the Persian Gulf conflict, and the options for altering the racial composition of the military.

Chapter 4 examines the increased prominence of reserve forces as a result of the total force policy and how well they served the nation in the Persian Gulf conflict. Their future roles are explored in light of the lessons of the conflict and the changes in the nature and magnitude of military threats in a post–cold war world. Chapter 5 summarizes findings and prescribes courses of action to help determine who will fight the next war.

Finally, this study focuses on the Army, for which these issues are most relevant. It is the largest military service, has the greatest concentration of African Americans in its ranks, the largest reserve component, and is the service for which the issue of women in combat is the most controversial. Where appropriate, I also discuss the experiences of the other services.

CHAPTER TWO

Women as Warriors?
Equal Opportunity and
National Security

HISTORICALLY, military service in the United States, as in most other nations, has been a masculine calling. The exploits of a few women who disguised themselves as men to serve in the nation's wars before the twentieth century have been widely chronicled, but except as nurses, the participation of women in the armed forces was not taken seriously until World War II, when 350,000 served. It was not until 1948 that women achieved a permanent military status.[1]

Even then their numbers were limited to not more than 2 percent of the total enlisted population, and the number of female officers was restricted to 10 percent of enlisted women.[2] The relatively few women who served were relegated largely to what was then considered women's work, mainly health care and administration. As recently as 1965, 93 percent of all enlisted women were serving in these occupations.[3]

---

1. For a more extended discussion of the historical role of women in the military, see Mattie E. Treadwell, *The Women's Army Corps* (Department of the Army, Office of the Chief of Military History, 1954); Jeanne Holm, *Women in the Military: An Unfinished Revolution*, rev. ed. (Novato, Calif.: Presidio Press, 1992); and Martin Binkin and Shirley J. Bach, *Women and the Military* (Brookings, 1977).
2. Women's Armed Services Integration Act of 1948. See 62 Stat. 357, 358.
3. Holm, *Women in the Military*, p. 184.

Expanding the Role of Women

The 2 percent limitation stood until 1967, when legislation altered provisions of the law that limited women's career opportunities and retirement provisions.[4] These changes were due, at least in part, to the efforts of a task force established by the Pentagon in 1966 to reassess the role of women in the armed forces and consider their "potential for greater employment, recruitment, and retention, especially in relation to current skill requirements of the buildup for Southeast Asia and other deployments."[5] Although couched in terms of military personnel requirements, the Pentagon study was also prompted by pressures brought by many women officers, emboldened by the feminist movement that was becoming a force in American society.

Still, women continued to make up less than 2 percent of the enlisted force for the rest of the decade. From 1948 through 1969, the percentage varied between 1.0 and 1.5 percent, averaging only 1.2 percent.[6] As late as 1970 there was little reason to believe that any significant expansion was being contemplated. The commission appointed by President Richard Nixon in 1969 to develop a plan for moving to an all-volunteer force examined a variety of alternatives for easing the task of attracting large numbers of qualified volunteers. As inconceivable as it now seems, it failed to consider expanding the participation of women, assuming that they would continue to constitute about 1.2 percent of the post-Vietnam force. The commission staff, in fact, even explored the possibility of substituting federal government civilian workers for military women to reduce budget outlays.[7] Responding fourteen years later to criticism of this oversight, the former director of the commission appeared apologetic.

> I was shocked to find [the] allegation that we gave no consideration to increasing the number of women in the military. I assure you, we were searching everywhere for a potential supply [of volunteers]. My shock led me to canvass my files in search of contradictory evidence. I could find no

4. 81 Stat. 374–84.

5. Holm, *Women in the Military*, p. 190.

6. Office of the Assistant Secretary of Defense, Comptroller, *Selected Manpower Statistics* (Department of Defense, May 1975), pp. 22, 46.

7. Ames S. Albro, Jr., "Civilian Substitution," *Studies Prepared for the President's Commission on an All-Volunteer Force*, vol. 1 (GPO, November 1970), p. 1-5-19.

record anywhere that we seriously considered the question of expanding the number of women in uniform.[8]

Regardless, when the services actually confronted replacing conscripts with volunteers, the magnitude of the challenge became evident and the possibility of increasing the number of women recruits was taken more seriously. A task force established by Secretary of Defense Melvin R. Laird in 1972 set out "to prepare contingency plans for increasing the use of women to offset possible shortages of male recruits after the end of the draft."[9]

Shortly after the study commenced, the Equal Rights Amendment cleared Congress, and although its vague contours left unclear its specific impact on the military, it did reinforce the impetus for change. Meanwhile, military women had instigated litigation charging that various military personnel policies were discriminatory. The results of the litigation were mixed, but women achieved a landmark victory in 1973 when the Supreme Court struck down the law that denied military women certain dependency benefits that were available to male personnel.[10]

The end of conscription and the women's rights movement thus helped reshape the armed forces. The impact can be measured by the growth in the number of women serving and the kinds of jobs they have been assigned.

Growth in Numbers

In 1972, when it became clear that limitations on the role of women in the armed forces were no longer tenable, some 45,000 comprised just 1.9 percent of all active-duty military personnel. By 1990 the number reached 226,000, 11 percent of the total. As figure 2-1 shows, most of the expansion occurred during the 1970s.

During the transition to an all-volunteer force (1972–76), the number of women on active duty more than doubled, reaching 109,000 or just

8. Comments of William H. Meckling in William Bowman, Roger Little, and G. Thomas Sicilia, eds., *The All-Volunteer Force after a Decade: Retrospect and Prospect* (Washington: Pergamon-Brassey's, 1986), p. 112.

9. Central All-Volunteer Task Force, "Utilization of Military Women (A Report of Increased Utilization of Military Women FY1973–1977)," Office of the Assistant Secretary of Defense for Manpower and Reserve Affairs, December 1972, p. i.

10. *Frontiero v. Richardson*, 411 U.S. 677 (1973). For a discussion of this case, see Binkin and Bach, *Women and the Military*, pp. 45–6; and Holm, *Women in the Military*, pp. 290–91.

Figure 2-1. *Women in the Armed Forces, Fiscal Years 1971–92*

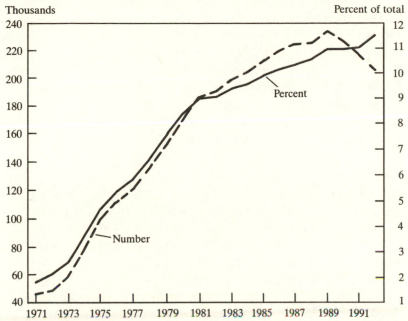

Source: Department of Defense, *Selected Manpower Statistics FY 1989* (1989), pp. 68–69, 100–01; 1990–92 data are from Defense Manpower Data Center.

over 5 percent of the force by the end of fiscal 1976. But the high growth rate started to slow in 1976 as the services reevaluated their policies and planned more gradual increases. Compared with the increase of 64,000 women that marked the first five years of the expansion, for the next five years, the Pentagon planned a growth rate of half that. Under the plan the proportion of women would have stabilized at 5 percent.

These plans, made in the closing months of the Ford administration, were challenged by the Carter administration, which wanted to emphasize equal opportunity. The Pentagon's civilian leadership was quick to pressure the armed forces to recruit more women, especially because the services were beginning to have difficulty attracting qualified male volunteers. In 1978 the services were directed to double the number of women in their ranks by 1983, when close to 200,000 enlisted women would comprise just over 11 percent of the force.[11] By the turn of the decade, 171,000 women were in the ranks, almost double the projection

11. Department of Defense, *Annual Report: Fiscal Year 1979*, p. 328.

made four years earlier. The final Carter administration plan, submitted in January 1981, projected increases to 265,000 by fiscal year 1986.[12]

The expanded numbers of women recruits not only enabled the armed forces to meet their quantitative goals but to help offset a dramatic deterioration in the quality of male recruits. From 1976 to 1980, Army recruits' level of education and entry test scores dropped to the lowest in recent memory: 38 percent were high school dropouts and 44 percent scored below the 31st percentile of all test takers. This development prompted some legislators to consider returning to conscription.[13] Matters would have been worse had it not been for women volunteers who were generally better educated and attained higher scores than men. For example, of the recruits who entered the Army between fiscal years 1974 and 1980, nearly 32 percent of the men scored in the lowest acceptable category on the standardized entry test compared with 15 percent of the women. The scores of less than 22 percent of the men were in the top third of the population, compared with more than 44 percent of the women.[14] The all-volunteer force might not have survived had it not been for the influx of highly qualified women.

With the change of administration in 1981, however, the Carter Pentagon's ambitious plans for further expanding the recruitment of women were put on hold, ostensibly to take stock.[15] The Reagan Pentagon justified the reevaluation on the grounds that "the increase [during the 1970s] was spurred primarily by social pressures for equal opportunity . . . [and] little effort was made during this period to empirically determine the best way to utilize women based on skill, mission, and readiness requirements."[16] The services, which had opposed the course—and the

---

12. Holm, *Women in the Military*, p. 387.

13. Martin Binkin, *America's Volunteer Military: Progress and Prospects* (Brookings, 1984), p. 9. These results were attributed in part to confusion about entry test scores. With the introduction of a new version of the standardized entry test in 1976, errors in converting raw test scores into percentile scores caused the latter to be overstated, thus qualifying many recruits who would otherwise have been ineligible. The error was significant: for example, in contrast to the original belief that only 5 percent of the recruits who entered the armed forces in fiscal year 1979 had scored in the lowest acceptable category, corrected scores placed 30 percent in that category. The Army was the most seriously affected. Nearly half its recruits, rather than 9 percent as reported originally scored below average. See Office of the Assistant Secretary of Defense, *Aptitude Testing of Recruits*, report to the House Committee on Armed Services (Department of Defense, 1980), p. 10.

14. Based on data obtained from the Defense Manpower Data Center.

15. Holm, *Women in the Military*, p. 385.

16. Office of the Assistant Secretary of Defense for Manpower, Reserve Affairs, and

Table 2-1. *Numbers of Women in the Military, by Service, Projected and Actual, Fiscal Year 1987*

Service	Projected		Actual
	Carter program	Reagan program	
Army	99,000	83,100	86,500
Navy	53,700	52,200	59,500
Marine Corps	9,600	9,700	9,700
Air Force	103,200	76,000	77,600
Total	265,500	221,000	233,300

Sources: Carter administration goals from Jeanne Holm, *Women in the Military: An Unfinished Revolution*, rev. ed. (Novato, Calif.: Presidio Press, 1992). Reagan administration goals from the Office of the Assistant Secretary of Defense for Manpower, Reserve Affairs, and Logistics.

pace—set by the Carter administration, anticipated that the new administration, less influenced by feminist pressures, would sanction and possibly encourage them to rethink their programs to recruit women. Besides, recruitment of qualified men took a turn for the better, thanks to increases in military pay, an economic recession, and improvements in the military's image, fostered in part by the nation's resonance with President Ronald Reagan's standing tall rhetoric.

The Army and Air Force, especially, were quick to alter their plans. One month after Reagan's inauguration, the Army announced its intention to reexamine the entire matter of women soldiers. In the meantime it would hold the line at 65,000 enlisted women. The Air Force revised its five-year projection, planning to have 61,000 rather than 90,000 women by 1987.[17] These changes, dubbed the womenpause by one critic,[18] were made without the blessings of the Pentagon's civilian bureaucracy and created consternation among military women and their congressional supporters. In early 1982, Secretary of Defense Caspar Weinberger, who turned out to be more supportive of the expansion than the services had expected, ordered an internal review of women in the military. The Army and Air Force subsequently increased their limits, but still projected goals for fiscal year 1987 roughly 40,000 less than the Carter administration had planned. As matters turned out, these new projections proved accurate (table 2-1).

Meanwhile, more women were also entering the military reserves. Growth was particularly evident in the Army Reserve, which by 1991 was

Logistics, *Military Women in the Department of Defense* (Department of Defense, April 1983), p. 1.
17. Holm, *Women in the Military*, p. 387.
18. Holm, *Women in the Military*, p. 387.

Figure 2-2. *Occupational Distribution of Enlisted Military Women, Fiscal Years 1972, 1990*

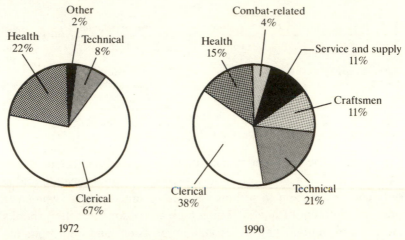

Source: Based on data from Defense Manpower Data Center.

20 percent women. The Army National Guard more than doubled its proportion of enlisted women between 1976 and 1991, from 2.7 to 7 percent, but remained behind the active army in absolute terms.[19] The difference between the Army's two reserve components stems in part from the contrasting missions of the organizations: the National Guard is composed principally of combat units and the Reserve mainly of support units.

Occupational Mix

Accompanying the increasing numbers of women in the military was a striking change in the duties they were assigned. In 1972, for example, more than 90 percent filled traditionally female medical and administrative positions, but by 1990 barely half were in those specialties. As figure 2-2 shows, many women now fill technical positions (for example, communications and intelligence), craftsmen's and mechanic's jobs, and service and supply billets.

19. Assistant Secretary of Defense for Manpower, Reserve Affairs, and Logistics, *Official Guard and Reserve Manpower Strengths and Statistics, June 1991*, report A6 (Department of Defense, 1991), pp. 1–6; and Office of the Deputy Chief of Staff for Personnel, *Equal Opportunity: Third Annual Assessment of Programs, March 1979* (Department of the Army, 1979), pp. 9–11.

And although restrictive laws and policies kept women out of combat, the definition of combat changed significantly. During the early days of the expansion, the services applied the strictest interpretation, precluding women from any duty that could by any stretch of the imagination be tied to combat. The Navy and Air Force were backed by statutory provisions embodied in the Women's Armed Services Integration Act of 1948, which provided that women "shall not be assigned to duty in aircraft while such aircraft are engaged in combat missions nor shall they be assigned to duty on vessels of the Navy except hospital ships and naval transports."[20]

Instead of placing similar restrictions on Army personnel, the act simply authorized the secretary of the Army to prescribe the kinds of military duty to which women could be assigned.[21] But with little doubt that Congress opposed assigning women to jobs that would expose them to danger or to duties considered physically too arduous, the Army adopted policies that prevented assigning women to units whose mission was related to combat or combat support. Thus in 1972, under the Army's definitions women could only be assigned to one-third of all Army units, within which about 19,000 enlisted positions were considered interchangeable, that is, they could be filled by either men or women.[22]

As the military received more women, however, and with signs that the expansion of their opportunities had to be taken seriously if the all-volunteer force was to succeed, the armed forces began to wrestle with the definition of combat. More seagoing billets were opened as the Navy placed some of its support fleet (tenders and combat logistics force ships, for example) in the noncombatant category. The Air Force permitted women to fly tanker, surveillance (AWACS), and cargo aircraft and, after

20. Women's Armed Services Integration Act of 1948, 62 Stat. 368, 373. Because there were no hospital or transport vessels in the fleet in the early 1970s, all seagoing jobs in the Navy were closed to women. Jobs on harbor craft and tugboats, however, which are not typically deployed on the high seas, were open to women. In 1976 about 300 women were assigned to these vessels. "Women in Navy: As Numbers Increase New Problems Arise," *Navy Times*, March 29, 1976, p. 15.

21. 62 Stat. 359. The Army preferred to have personnel assignment authority vested in the secretary of the Army, citing the need for flexibility with anticipated changes in doctrine and tactics and associated combat skills. See "Testimony by Colonel Mary Hallaren," *Women's Armed Services Integration Act of 1947*, Hearings before the Senate Armed Services Committee, 80 Cong. 1 sess. (Government Printing Office, 1947), p. 88.

22. Office of the Deputy Chief of Staff for Personnel, "Women in the Army Study" (Department of the Army, December 1, 1976), pp. 5-2, 5-3.

a prolonged and emotional debate, to be launch officers for its intercontinental ballistic missile force.[23]

The Army, however, had the greatest struggle. Initially it modified its restrictions so that by 1977 women were excluded from only thirty-one combat skills. They were also excluded from units whose primary mission included engaging and inflicting casualties or equipment damage on the enemy. Moreover, the Army developed an elaborate formula for limiting the number of women as a function of a unit's expected proximity to the battlefield. By this logic, the Army maintained it could accommodate about 50,000 women soldiers (curiously identical to the goal it had established in 1972) and 9,000 women officers.[24]

By the end of the 1980s, Army policy excluded women from routine engagement in direct combat, defined as "engaging an enemy with individual or crew-served weapons while being exposed to direct enemy fire, a high probability of direct physical contact with the enemy's personnel, and a substantial risk of capture. Direct combat takes place while closing with the enemy by fire, maneuver, or shock effect in order to destroy or capture, or while repelling assault by fire, close combat, or counterattack."[25]

The services' rules for assigning women to combat-related duties were standardized by a Pentagon task force on women in 1988, which developed a risk rule that noncombat units could be "closed to women on grounds of risks of exposure to direct combat, hostile fire, or capture provided that the type, degree, and duration of such risks *are equal to or greater than* that experienced by combat units in the same theater of operations."[26] But there were still enough ambiguities in the definition of combat to allow the services wide latitude in establishing assignment policies.[27]

By 1990 more than half of all Army positions, 60 percent of those in the Navy, and 97 percent of those in the Air Force were considered gender

23. It is somewhat ironic that the Air Force permitted women to fly tankers but not bombers; tankers would be at least as desirable a target for an enemy.

24. Office of Deputy Chief of Staff for Personnel, "Women in the Army Study," chaps. 3, 5.

25. Carolyn Becraft, "Women in the U.S. Armed Services: The War in the Persian Gulf," fact sheet (Women's Research and Education Institute, March 1991), p. 4.

26. Becraft, "Women in the U.S. Armed Services," p. 4.

27. Retired Air Force Major General Jeanne Holm refers to this as the Humpty Dumpty factor, contending that the services, like Humpty Dumpty in *Through the Looking Glass*, could use the term combat to mean whatever they chose it to mean. See *Women in the Military*, p. 398.

neutral. In contrast, only 20 percent of Marine Corps jobs were open to women because the Corps has the highest ratio of combat to support positions. And many support services, such as medical care, that the other services provide for themselves are provided for the Marine Corps by the Navy.[28]

Occupational changes also accompanied the expanded numbers of women in the reserve forces, but women reservists were not as successful in making inroads into nontraditional occupations. In the Army Reserve, for example, 55 percent still hold jobs in health or administration, and 63 percent in the Army National Guard fill those billets.[29]

Tackling Discrimination

Beyond questions of numbers and jobs, many practices that discriminated against military women have also been altered. The pace of change was especially dramatic during the 1970s as "one by one . . . the barriers toppled over, sometimes catapulted by sweeping decisions, more often downed by the laborious process of studies, tests, hearings, and litigation."[30] The more obvious discriminatory policies were the first to be changed. Women with children were no longer automatically discharged, and family entitlements for married servicemen and servicewomen were equalized. Women were allowed to command aviation maintenance units and similar organizations. They were enrolled for the first time in ROTC programs, and they were given wider access to weapons training. In 1976, after a good deal of emotional debate, the services admitted women into the military academies.

In one of the most significant changes, pregnant women were no longer forced to leave the military. Restrictions in place since 1951 had permitted the services to terminate women as they became pregnant. Although the order was permissive, each service accepted it as a mandate, and it stood mostly unchallenged until the early 1970s. Following several legal challenges and after urgings by the Pentagon's civilian leadership, the services slowly established more liberal waiver policies.

The Air Force led the way in 1971, providing for "waivers of discharge, reentry within twelve months for women who were discharged, and cancellation of discharge action when a pregnancy was terminated by mis-

28. Becraft, "Women in the U.S. Armed Services," p. 4.
29. Data provided by Defense Manpower Data Center.
30. Holm, *Women in the Military*, p. 267.

carriage or abortion."[31] The other services followed suit, some more reluctantly than others. The Army held out the longest. Brigadier General Mildred C. Bailey, director of the Women's Army Corps, explained, "Mothers have a role in child rearing that is different from fathers and we have to think about what effect this has on mission readiness and our ability to be available for world-wide assignment. . . . It is unthinkable that a pregnant woman should continue to live in troop billets, sharing rooms and facilities with her peers during the advanced stages of pregnancy."[32] The courts became involved in 1976, when the Second Circuit Court ruled that regulations requiring women to be discharged as soon as pregnancy was discovered violated the Fifth Amendment.[33]

Under current regulations, women who become pregnant during basic training are immediately discharged. Those who become pregnant after basic training may request to be discharged.[34] The request can be denied if a woman has accepted enlistment or reenlistment bonuses, has incurred an obligation after receiving training or education, or holds a critical or hard-to-fill occupation. Those who remain face assignment restrictions that vary among the services. In the Army pregnant women are ineligible for overseas assignment except to accompany military spouses, assuming there is an appropriate assignment for them. Those in the Marine Corps, however, are eligible for worldwide assignment until the sixth week of pregnancy, after which travel is prohibited.

The Final Barrier

As the expansion of the number of women and the kinds of jobs they could fill slowed in the 1980s, so too did much of the controversy that had surrounded the issue of women in combat. By the end of the 1980s, servicewomen seemed more intent on preserving hard-won gains than on urging further expansion. Their attention turned toward improving their opportunities for command and promotion and eliminating the incidents of sexual harassment that appeared to be on the increase.

The nettlesome question of women in combat arose now and then, only to meet the continued resistance of the Pentagon leadership and

31. Holm, *Women in the Military*, p. 300.
32. Holm, *Women in the Military*, pp. 300–01.
33. *Crawford* v. *Cushman*, 531 F.2d 114 (2d Cir., 1976).
34. These conditions are summarized in "Parental Leave in the U.S. Military," fact sheet published by the Women's Equity Action League in 1988.

most legislators. The many arguments against placing women in combat jobs, which have been present since the beginning of the debate, can be grouped as follows:

—Women do not possess the physical strength to perform rigorous combat duties, especially in infantry and armor positions.

—Women have not been socialized to be violent; they do not possess the emotional characteristics to handle the stresses of the battlefield.

—The presence of women in combat units would interfere with the male bonding considered vital to unit cohesion, foster fraternization and harassment, and compromise unit effectiveness.

—The financial costs associated with modifications necessary to provide privacy and compatibility for women would be prohibitive.

—The American people are not prepared to see their daughters, sisters, wives, or mothers die in combat or be taken prisoner.

—The nation is not ready to accept the conscription of women nor allow them to be assigned *involuntarily* to combat jobs as their male counterparts would be under wartime mobilization conditions.

The issue of women in combat, however, attracted less and less attention as the 1980s drew to a close. As prospects for combat assignments dwindled, passions waned among those who had been identified with trying to remove restrictions. Among servicewomen, the most vocal supporters were officers, but even their enthusiasm seemed to dampen. And leaders of the civilian feminist movement who have always been ambivalent toward the military, were not inclined to take up this particular crusade.[35]

By the turn of the decade the residual pressure, such as it was, came from Representative Patricia Schroeder of Colorado, an influential member of the House Armed Services Committee, and several outspoken commentators, such as Carolyn Becraft, a former Army officer and consultant for the Women's Research and Education Institute. But even they seemed to stop short of advocating that ground combat positions be opened. While these women deserve much of the credit for promoting

---

35. The feminist movement has always walked a tightrope on the issue of women and the military. Generally, feminists tend to be pacifists, and strong support of an expanded role for women in the armed forces might appear to dignify the military establishment. Many, too, probably remember that the failure to obtain ratification of the ERA in the mid-1970s was attributed by some to fears that the amendment would make women liable for military service. See, for example, Joan M. Krauskopf, "The Equal Rights Amendment: Its Political and Practical Contexts," *California State Bar Journal*, vol. 50 (March-April 1975), p. 136.

the interests of servicewomen, they had seemingly run against a wall in their attempts to integrate this last male refuge.

Interest was renewed in 1987 when the Canadian minister of defense announced plans to evaluate the operational effectiveness of combat units composed of both men and women through experiments involving infantry, field and air-defense artillery, armored corps, field engineers, signals (communications), naval operations, and fighter air operations, all of which were closed to women. According to a Canadian defense official, the results were mixed. "Most of the women who have undertaken naval or combat arms training courses have had no difficulty in meeting the required standards. The one major exception is in infantry training. Only one woman, of the 47 who have entered this training, has met the rigorous standards required to pass. Conversely, those who have been trained in armour, artillery and signals have fared much better."[36]

In 1989 the U.S. Defense Advisory Committee on Women in the Services (DACOWITS) called for a similar four-year test of women in Army combat units, but enabling legislation submitted by Representative Schroeder in 1990 died. A year later, DACOWITS acknowledged defeat and dropped its demand.[37] Clearly, the constituency for women in combat, especially ground combat, was too small to force such a dramatic change. Besides, with the end of the cold war and the anticipated reductions in the armed forces, most military women were preoccupied with whether they might be squeezed out of the armed services entirely. These fears, however, had not materialized by fiscal year 1992, when the proportion of women reached a record 11.5 percent (figure 2-1). Indeed, total military strength decreased faster than the number of military women.

Interest in allowing women into combat was revived again in January 1990 when the Pentagon confirmed that Captain Linda Bray had commanded a unit in the U.S. invasion of Panama. An administration official called it "the first time that a woman has commanded Americans in

36. Speech by the Honorable Mary Collins, PC, MP, Canadian associate minister of national defence, to the Western European Defence Committee, July 26, 1990, in "The Role of Women in the Armed Forces," Assembly of Western European Union, thirty-seventh ordinary session, first part, document 1267, May 13, 1991, p. 38. The tests were overtaken by events in February 1989 when the Canadian Human Rights Tribunal directed the Canadian armed forces to remove any remaining employment restrictions based on sex, with the exception of duty on submarines.

37. Grant Willis, "DACOWITS Drops Press for Army Test of Women in Combat," *Army Times*, November 5, 1990, p. 12.

Table 2-2. *Deployment of Military Personnel to the Persian Gulf Area, by Service and Gender, August 1990–February 1991*

Service	Men	Women	Total	Women as percent of total
Army	287,656	30,855	318,511	9.69
Navy	101,241	4,449	105,690	4.21
Marine Corps	83,022	1,232	84,254	1.46
Air Force	56,584	4,246	60,830	6.98
Total	528,503	40,782	569,285	7.16

Source: Mark J. Eitelberg, "Preliminary Assessment of Population Representation in Operations Desert Shield and Desert Storm," paper prepared for the 1991 Biennial Conference of the Inter-University Seminar on Armed Forces and Society.

battle."[38] Although the circumstances were clarified and the event's significance played down in subsequent reports, the participation of some 120 women in Operation Just Cause served as a reminder that the distinctions between combat and support positions were blurred and, given the changes in technology and warfighting doctrine and tactics, were becoming even more so.[39]

Lessons of the Persian Gulf Conflict

When the military forces of the United States were sent to the Persian Gulf in August 1990, the largest deployment of women to a combat zone since World War II commenced, and the first major test of America's all-volunteer force was under way. More than 40,000 military women served in the Persian Gulf region during Operations Desert Shield and Desert Storm, accounting for over 7 percent of all U.S. troops deployed. The deployments varied by service (table 2-2), with most being Army women.

38. Michael R. Gordon, "For First Time, A Woman Leads G.I.'s in Combat," *New York Times*, January 4, 1990, p. A13.

39. Michael R. Gordon, "U.S. Tells Calmer Story of Woman's Role in Commanding Attack," *New York Times*, January 9, 1990, p. A15. Captain Bray had commanded a military police unit that captured a dog kennel run by the Panamanian Defense Force. Because the operation was blown so far out of proportion by the media, according to Captain Bray, she was subjected to ridicule and harassment within the Army. She accepted a medical discharge in April 1991, having suffered stress fractures on both legs "because of marching with a heavy pack in training." See Peter Copeland, "Back to the Kitchen: Publicity of Panama Cost Captain Her Career," *Washington Times*, July 1, 1991, p. 1. The irony of the situation was not lost on those critics who have contended that most women could not cope with the physical demands of combat training. Captain Bray herself expressed doubts about women serving in the infantry because of the physical requirements.

Figure 2-3. *Occupational Representation of Women Deployed to Operations Desert Shield and Desert Storm, 1990–91*

Percent

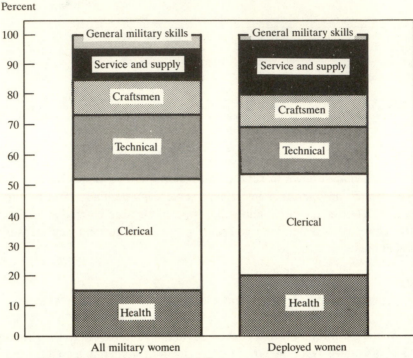

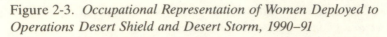

Source: Based on data from Defense Manpower Data Center.

Of these women, 27,000 were active duty and the rest reservists. Women accounted for more than 13 percent of reservists mobilized for the campaign but less than 7 percent of active duty personnel.

In earlier conflicts, women filled medical and administrative positions almost exclusively. But those in the Persian Gulf war served in virtually all military occupations permitted under existing laws and policies. With minor exceptions, the jobs were representative of their assignments in the peacetime military (figure 2-3).

The deployment of women to the Persian Gulf attracted widespread news coverage. National television audiences were treated to nightly images of American servicewomen preparing for war in desert camouflage fatigues under the same austere and seemingly dangerous conditions as their male counterparts. Once the battle was joined, the public saw women flying and maintaining aircraft, driving supply vehicles along the

Saudi-Kuwait border, running prisoner-of-war facilities, and launching Patriot missiles at incoming Scuds.

These circumstances were watched closely by people on both sides of the women-in-combat issue. At last, many hoped, the debate could be elevated from the emotional rhetoric of the past two decades to objective analysis based on observed performance in an actual war and could finally provide answers to some nagging questions: How would women cope under rigorous and dangerous field conditions? How would their presence affect men? How would the nation react to women being killed, wounded, or taken prisoner?

The Evidence

There was no organized effort to evaluate the performance of American military personnel in general or women in particular during the Persian Gulf conflict. Any conclusions, therefore, rest mostly on anecdotal information provided by military sources or obtained through observation and interviews. To be sure, the news media were crucial in highlighting—and in some cases overdramatizing—women's participation. But even allowing for possible media exaggerations and distortions and acknowledging the limitations on inferences to be drawn from this conflict, some conclusions can be reached.

First, many women were exposed to the arduous field conditions critics contended they would be unable to handle. There was little to indicate, however, that women were any less able than men to cope with primitive sanitary arrangements, lack of privacy, isolation, boredom, and the other deprivations involved with their deployment.

Second, the experience in the Persian Gulf conflict, while limited, further supports the argument that changes in modern warfare have made many combat and support functions not easily distinguishable. Precision-guided, long-range munitions and military tactics that emphasized attacking rear areas to disrupt critical lines of communication, it has been argued, render entire theaters of military operations combat zones. Thus restricting women to support duties does not take them out of harm's way. Indeed, it could put them in a combat situation without the training and means to defend themselves.[40]

40. Concerns about the vulnerabilities of rear support troops have been based mostly on the Soviet threat. Combat scenarios for Central Europe envisaged Soviet tactics, backed

Of the 375 total U.S. deaths in Operations Desert Shield and Desert Storm from August 1990 through February 1991, 211 (56 percent) were among personnel assigned to support duties.[41] Twenty-eight resulted when an Iraqi Scud hit a temporary barracks in Dhahran, Saudi Arabia. The distinction between combat and support was further narrowed in the public's eye when Major Marie Rossi piloted a CH-47 cargo helicopter into the battle-zone in support of the Army's 101st Airborne (Air Assault) Division shortly after the war started.[42]

Third, against many critics' contentions that Americans are unprepared to accept the idea of women being sent home in body bags or taken prisoner, the public seemed no more appalled by the reports of female casualties and POWs than by the reports of men being killed or taken prisoner. Among the 375 U.S. fatalities, 13 were women and of 25 American prisoners of war, two were women:[43] Army Specialist Melissa Rathbun-Nealy, a truck driver captured near the Saudi town of Khafji; and Major Rhonda Cornum, an Army flight surgeon taken prisoner when a Black Hawk helicopter on a medical evacuation mission was shot down over Iraq.

Treatment of American women prisoners was a subject of considerable interest. Speculation through the years had considered that they might be sexually attacked. Soon after the end of the conflict, Major Cornum allayed those concerns.

> People ask me all the time how I was treated. My answer is, probably not as badly as people who were captured in January. And since we were the first people to be taken prisoner by our Iraqi unit, not as badly as we treated the Iraqi POWs.
>
> I have also been asked by our people if I was treated differently because I was a woman. Well, not really—other than they all looked away when they took my uniform off of me.[44]

---

up with deep-strike weapons, that would strike many priority targets behind the front lines. Although Iraq possessed aircraft and long-range weapons that could have targeted rear areas, only the Scuds were employed for this purpose.

41. Mark J. Eitelberg, "Preliminary Assessment of Population Representation in Operations Desert Shield and Desert Storm," paper prepared for the 1991 Biennial Conference of the Inter-University Seminar on Armed Forces and Society.

42. Major Rossi was killed in a noncombat accident the day following the cease-fire. Robert D. McFadden, "New Jersey Pilot, A Woman, Dies in Crash in Gulf," *New York Times*, March 4, 1991, p. B2.

43. Eitelberg, "Preliminary Assessment."

44. Gilbert Cranberg, "Disinformation on Women POWs," *USA Today*, June 16, 1992, p. 13A.

In testimony before the Presidential Commission on the Assignment of Women in the Armed Forces a year later, however, Major Cornum revised her account; she had been "violated manually, vaginally and rectally" by an Iraqi soldier.[45] The commission was also informed by an Army official that Rathbun-Nealy had been "the victim of indecent assaults," a charge she apparently has denied.[46]

The Persian Gulf operation also provided the first opportunity to gather information on gender-related medical fitness, especially the effects of pregnancy on deployability and military readiness. The Pentagon reported that nearly one of every ten women considered for deployment was not deployed for medical reasons, half of them because of pregnancy. Only 2 percent of men were categorized as nondeployable for medical reasons. Of those personnel who were deployed, 2.5 percent of the women and 2 percent of the men returned to the United States earlier than their units for a variety of medical and administrative reasons.[47]

All in all, the Persian Gulf experience was considered a major accomplishment for military women, who won virtually unanimous respect among their male military commanders and peers and from the American people. As one woman Army officer reported, "in Desert Storm, we experienced a new kind of relationship between men and women. There was real professional respect. We went through the same things. We pulled together in conditions that were worse than horrible."[48]

More important, although women did not participate in combat operations per se, the experience held significant implications for that issue as well. After military women returning from the Gulf contended the conflict "should have dispelled notions that they are not qualified for

45. Rowan Scarborough, "Female POWs Molested," Washington Times, June 12, 1992, p. 1. The reasons for the disparities in the two accounts are unclear, but Major Cornum dismissed the ordeal as "an occupational hazard of going to war." The Pentagon, for its part, denied covering up the abusive treatment of female POWs, indicating that any discussion of the specifics had been left to the women involved, since they were the ones who suffered. "They ought to be the ones to decide how much is said."

46. Scarborough, "Female POWs Molested," p. 1. Her denial is referred to in Presidential Commission on the Assignment of Women in the Armed Forces, Report to the President, November 15, 1992 (1992), p. C-44.

47. Department of Defense, "Utilization of American Military Women in Operations Desert Shield and Desert Storm, August 2, 1990 to April 11, 1991" (July 29, 1992). A fairer comparison would include personnel who were not deployed for any reason, but those data were not included in this report.

48. Army Captain Carol Barkalow, quoted in Ellen Goodman, "Women and War: Time Law Caught Up with Fact," Baltimore Sun, April 23, 1991, p. 7.

combat," the Defense Advisory Committee on Women in the Services established as its top priority the removal of combat exclusion laws.[49]

Congress Reacts

It did not take long for the small circle of proponents on Capitol Hill to exploit the postwar euphoria. Two weeks after the DACOWITS proposal, as the House Armed Services Committee considered the 1992 defense authorization bill, Representative Pat Schroeder sponsored legislation to lift the exclusion that prohibited women from serving as combat aviators in the Air Force. (The Air Force had earlier hinted it would be willing to cooperate.) In a surprise move Representative Beverly Byron of Maryland, chair of the Military Personnel Subcommittee and a legislator who had long opposed the idea of women in combat, extended the proposal to cover the Navy. Byron attributed her change of heart to the experiences of women in the Persian Gulf: "we had women . . . that were in a threatened environment, that were in a hostile environment, in a front-line environment. . . . I don't perceive [the amendment] as that monumental. To me, it was just a logical next step."[50] The measure was pushed through the committee without a public hearing or a public vote.

The legislation subsequently cleared the full House without debate. Lawmakers sought to avoid recorded votes and open floor debates, according to one report, for fear of offending feminists on one hand or the military leadership on the other.[51] The Pentagon's civilian leadership was surprisingly supportive. As spokesman Pete Williams said, "our view about the legislation is it's beneficial, it's a good thing, we support it because it gives the Department of Defense the authority to make these decisions."[52]

Especially noteworthy, and perhaps crucial to the swiftness of the House action, were the signals sent by an unlikely source, Senator John

49. Bernard Adelsberger, "DACOWITS: 'What Else Do We Have to Do?'" *Army Times*, September 23, 1991, p. 18.

50. Tom Bowman, "Byron's Stance on Women in Combat Has Softened," *Baltimore Sun*, May 13, 1991, p. 1.

51. Rowan Scarborough, "Decision Near on Women in Combat," *Washington Times*, May 22, 1991, p. 1.

52. Quoted in "Resistance to Women in Combat Appears Strong in Naval Aviation Community," *Inside the Navy*, September 16, 1991, p. 1.

McCain, a ranking Republican on the Senate Armed Services Committee. During a hearing of the Subcommittee on Manpower and Personnel in April 1991, he contended that, given their performance in the Gulf, the policy excluding women from combat needed to be reevaluated. Though stopping short of suggesting that ground combat duties might be appropriate, McCain said he saw "no reason women should not be allowed to serve in Navy combatant ships, as Navy and Air Force fighter pilots and as helicopter pilots on combat missions in the Army and Marine Corps."[53]

Caught off guard by the speed of the House action, opponents of the measure marshalled forces in time to influence the Senate Armed Services Committee, which scheduled hearings on the issue in mid-June. As a result of testimony by military leaders and both male and female members of the armed forces, along with lobbying efforts by conservatives such as Phyllis Schlafly of the Eagle Forum and Elaine Donnelly of the Coalition for Military Readiness, the committee was reluctant to endorse the House legislation.[54]

Critics of the House measure apparently raised second thoughts among senators. Some worried that repealing the restrictions would ultimately lead to assigning women to ground combat roles; others were concerned about the cost of remodeling ships to accommodate female personnel. Still others feared that women would become subject to registration and, if necessary, conscription. Some senators speculated that opening combat jobs to women would diminish their propensity to volunteer for military service. The testimony by military service members reinforced the conventional wisdom that women officers are more likely than their enlisted counterparts to favor combat assignments and male sailors and airmen are more willing to serve with women in combat than are male soldiers and marines.[55]

53. Rick Maze, "Sen. McCain: It's Time to Remove Assignment Restrictions," *Navy Times*, May 6, 1991, p. 3.

54. Schlafly reportedly was responsible for converting Representative Robert Dornan of California, who had initially voted in committee for striking down the combat restrictions. Rowan Scarborough, "Momentum Slows to Allow Women in Combat Aircraft," *Washington Times*, July 1, 1991, p. A11. See also, Phyllis Schlafly, "Feminist Combat Maneuver," *Washington Times*, May 21, 1991, p. G4; and Barton Gellman, "Combat Role for Women Stalled by Senate Panel," *Washington Post*, July 10, 1991, p. A4.

55. Rick Maze, "Fear of Open Floodgates Stalls Combat Bid," *Army Times*, July 1, 1991, p. 8.

Accordingly, the Senate committee took a cautious approach.

> The quest to sanction the assignment of women to combat skills and positions raises basic questions about the future shape and structure of the armed forces that cannot be answered by merely opening selected combat skills and positions to women or by giving the Secretary of Defense discretionary authority to make the decision.[56]

Recognizing that the issue involved both military and social considerations, the committee continued, "The nation must make such decisions openly, deliberately, and after a full examination of all the available facts. It must neither continue the current combat restriction laws and policies for invalid reasons, nor repeal such laws or policies without a full understanding of the effect and meaning of such action."

Accordingly, the committee recommended forming a fifteen-member presidential commission to study all aspects of the issues before making any changes in the law. The full Senate, however, also accepted an amendment cosponsored by Senators William Roth of Delaware and Edward Kennedy of Massachusetts that essentially mirrored the House bill by allowing the secretaries of the military services to set policy guidelines for women's duties. The Senate bill, therefore, provided both for removing the restrictions on combat flying and for establishing the commission. In conference, the Senate deferred to the House wording on the removal of the combat restrictions and the House deferred to the Senate position on establishing the commission.

The commission was directed to study and report on, at a minimum, the following issues:

The combat readiness and effectiveness implications of opening some or all combat skills and positions to women.

—What are the physical requirements for each combat skill or position, including the full implications of gender norming?

—What is the impact of pregnancy and child care on assignment policies for military personnel?

—What is the practical effect of opening combat skills and positions to women on unit morale and cohesion?

The degree of public support for opening some or all combat skills and positions to women.

—Should combat assignments for women be voluntary or compulsory to the same extent such assignments are compulsory for men?

---

56. *National Defense Authorization Act for Fiscal Years 1992 and 1993*, report 102–113, Senate Armed Services Committee, 102 Cong. 1 sess. (GPO, 1991), p. 217.

—Should women be required to register and be subject to the draft on the same basis as men if women have the same opportunity as men to compete for all skills and positions in the military?

The legal and constitutional implications of opening some or all combat skills and positions to women.

—If current combat exclusion laws are repealed, but the Military Services retain the discretion to prescribe combat assignment restrictions for women, how will this affect the constitutionality of the male-only registration and service requirements of the Military Selective Service Act?

—If current combat exclusion laws and policies are repealed, would the present policy under which only males may be involuntarily assigned to combat skills and positions be sustainable?

The requirements and costs of modifying weapons systems to accommodate women for habitability and anthropomorphic reasons if some or all combat skills and positions are opened to women.

—What would be the impact of required changes in quarters, weapons, training, and what would be the costs of such changes?

—What would be the practical rate at which any required changes can be made in an era of severely constrained defense budgets?[57]

The establishment of the commission, as matters turned out, provided the Pentagon with a rationale for delaying the admission of women into combat flight training; it announced that no changes would be made until the commission completed a year-long study. Contending that this stance circumvented the intent of Congress, which "clearly signaled the Pentagon to immediately let women start competing for combat flier slots," Representative Schroeder characterized the delay as "an insult to women."[58]

Issues and Options

Many of the questions considered by the commission have been raised before, and several have been subjects of close study. Others have been extremely difficult to analyze in the absence of data and methods for measuring military readiness, effectiveness, and unit cohesion. Public

57. *National Defense Authorization Act*, pp. 217–18.
58. Rowan Scarborough, "Byron, Schroeder Rip Delay on Pilots," *Washington Times*, December 5, 1991, p. 3.

attitudes toward women and the military have been gauged from time to time, but almost always during peacetime. In anticipation that the Persian Gulf experience may have yielded fresh data, it is therefore appropriate to raise the questions again.

Combat Readiness and Effectiveness

Critics have argued that allowing women to serve in combat units would degrade the readiness and effectiveness of those units. Most women, so this argument goes, do not possess the physical or emotional attributes necessary for combat. Their introduction into traditional combat activities would also upset the male bonding vital to unit cohesion, and the physical limitations and restricted assignments deriving from pregnancies would disrupt the readiness and effectiveness of the units.

PHYSICAL CAPABILITIES. Despite the continuing debate over whether women possess the physical characteristics necessary for combat assignments, the physical standards for specific military jobs have been neither well defined nor rigorously applied.[59] Each service has established standards that apply once a person has been trained and is on the job. But except for the Air Force, applicants are not required to demonstrate any measure of physical strength before they enter the armed forces, basic training, or specific job training. Prevailing doctrine has assumed that people able to meet minimum medical standards would also be able to meet prescribed levels of physical fitness during basic military training. Skill training courses leading to qualifications for specific job specialties would also reveal physical deficiencies.

The system worked for many years with the tacit understanding that the stronger members of a unit would take care of physically demanding duties beyond the abilities of the less robust members. This practice went unchallenged until the 1970s when women were assigned to nontraditional jobs for which certain levels of strength were needed. Women's physical capabilities have attracted even more attention as the possibility is pondered of assigning them to the most physically demanding of military tasks—ground combat duty.

The examination given to ascertain whether people meet prescribed medical standards for entry into military service consists of a clinical

59. Although physical fitness is not precisely defined, it is usually considered to encompass some combination of strength, endurance, flexibility, balance, speed, agility, and power.

examination of the body, laboratory findings, physical measurements (height, weight, blood pressure), a summary of defects and diagnoses, the physician's subjective determination of military fitness, the identification of disqualifying defects, and an evaluation of the person's functional capacity.[60]

The entry standards applied to men and women are similar except for weight. The weight of prospective recruits is calculated in terms of body-mass, which "combines height and weight into a common metric that correlates well with more comprehensive measures of body fat."[61] By common medical standards, 14 percent of men and women in the 17- to 22-year-old population would be considered overweight. Military standards are not rigorously applied, but they are more liberal for men, with the result that the armed forces exclude five times as many young women as young men. For example, during fiscal years 1982-85, more than 20 percent of Army male recruits exceeded the civilian medical overweight standards, with 8 percent twenty pounds or more overweight, while 1 percent of Army female recruits exceeded the standard, with most less than five pounds overweight.[62] It has been suggested that the more stringent standards for women are the result of an overabundance of women applicants.[63]

60. Army Regulation 40–501, "Medical Services Standards of Medical Fitness," May 15, 1989, pp. 80–87; and interim change 101, October 1, 1991.

61. Richard Buddin, *Weight Problems and Attrition of High-Quality Military Recruits*, N-2847-FMP (Santa Monica, Calif.: RAND, 1989), p. 1. Buddin points out that military standards differ from common epidemiological standards, which define men as overweight if their bodymass or weight-height index is equal to or greater than 26 kg/m^2 and women as overweight if their index is equal to or greater than 32 kg/m$^{1.5}$.

62. Buddin, *Weight Problems*, pp. 2–4. Buddin notes that some differences may be appropriate since medical standards are used to screen health risks, while military standards are geared more to the physical demands of military service.

63. Mark J. Eitelberg, *Manpower for Military Occupations* (Office of the Assistant Secretary of Defense for Force Management and Personnel, April 1988), p. 109. Eitelberg also cited a practice, now discontinued, that applied standards of appearance to women applicants. An author of a vocational guidance handbook described the so-called no uglies test: "As incredible as it may seem, until a few years ago one of the unofficial criteria for a woman to enter the military was that she be attractive! Recruiters were required to submit a full-length photograph of the female applicant to headquarters. There, all the female applicants' qualifications were compared—including how physically attractive they were—and a decision was made on which female would be permitted to enlist." See Texe W. Marrs, *You and the Armed Forces* (Arco Publishing, 1983), p. 23. Jeanne Holm also reported that in 1966, "the Air Force Chief of Staff admonished the commander of the Recruiting Service to get 'better looking WAF' [Women in the Air Force] . . . each applicant was required to pose for four photographs: front, side, back, and full-face . . . it was a beauty contest, and

The evaluation of functional capacity—the physician's subjective assessment of a person's ability to perform military duties—is quantified through a "physical profile," an index of overall functional capacity used to communicate an examinee's general physical condition to nonmedical personnel. The profile consists of six factors (commonly called the PULHES) representing the major human functions: physical capacity or stamina, upper extremities, lower extremities, hearing and ear defects, eyes, and psychiatric stability.

The factors are graded on a numerical scale from 1 to 4. Grade 1 signifies a high level of medical fitness; for example, with respect to "physical capacity" it indicates a person with good muscular development who can "perform at maximum effort" for indefinite periods. Grade 2 indicates some medical condition or physical defect that may impose certain job limitations; this grade would be assigned to someone who was "able to perform at maximum effort over long periods." Grade 3 applies to those with a "moderate" defect; it would be given to a person unable to perform at maximum effort except for brief or moderate periods. Grade 4 would indicate that a person was below minimum standards for enlistment.

Scores assigned to each factor combine to form a profile serial number. Under current Army personnel procurement standards, two categories are acceptable for peacetime duty. Those people with a PULHES profile serial 111111, signifying no demonstrable anatomical or physiological impairments within established standards, are considered medically fit and can generally be assigned without limitations. Those whose profile serial contains a grade 2 as the lowest designator—for example, slightly limited mobility of joints or muscular weakness—are considered combat fit with no significant assignment limitations. In general, grade 3 or 4 assigned to any factor is disqualifying for initial entrance but acceptable for someone already in the service.

Special profiling provisions are made for pregnant soldiers. Upon confirmation of pregnancy the medical authority issues a new profile, which at a minimum assigns a special code T-3 to the physical stamina P factor. This profile indicates the following limitations:

—Except under unusual circumstances, the soldier should not be reassigned to or from overseas commands until the pregnancy is terminated.

---

the commander of the Recruiting Service was the final judge." *Women in the Military*, p. 181.

—The soldier is exempted from the regular PT program of the unit, physical fitness testing, wearing load bearing equipment (including web belt), and exposure to chemical agents in nuclear, biological, chemical (NBC) training.

—At twenty weeks of pregnancy, the soldier is exempt from standing at parade rest or attention for longer than fifteen minutes and is exempt from participating in weapons training, swimming qualifications, and field duty.

—No assignment will be made to duties where nausea, easy fatigability, or sudden lightheadedness would be hazardous, including all aviation duty.[64]

The relationship between medical examination results and physical requirements associated with specific jobs has varied by service. The Army associates a profile serial with each occupational specialty. Entrance into infantry training, for example, requires a perfect 111111. A 222221 profile may be acceptable for missile electronics repair, a job less physically demanding than infantry duty, and one in which some minor defects are acceptable in all factors except psychiatric. Among enlisted soldiers who entered the Army between 1987 and 1991 and for whom records are available, an equal proportion of men and women (73 percent) possessed a perfect profile. Under current standards they would be considered physically qualified for infantry training.[65] This unrealistically high rate of women qualifying underscores the limitations of relying on the PULHES profile for assessing physical capabilities and indicates that direct measurements of physical strength and stamina are needed.

Recognizing these shortcomings, the Air Force has since the mid-1970s administered to all prospective recruits a physical strength test, which involves lifting various weights, from 40 to 200 pounds, to a height of six feet. To qualify for enlistment, applicants must lift 40 pounds; to qualify for specific occupations, they may be required to lift heavier amounts. For example, to enter training as a refrigeration and air conditioning specialist, one of the most physically demanding skills, an applicant must lift 110 pounds to six feet.[66]

64. Army Regulation 40-501, interim change I01, p. 3.
65. Data provided by Defense Manpower Data Center, April 1992.
66. The test uses an incremental weight machine that requires a person to bend over and lift a bar, much as one would lift a barbell from a standing position. The initial weight setting is 40 pounds, with weights added in 10-pound increments, up to a maximum of 200 pounds, until the applicant cannot complete a valid lift. Data provided by Department of

In 1984 the Army implemented a similar program, the Military Entrance Physical Strength Capacity Test (MEPSCAT), to assess strength and stamina and predict performance on tasks relevant to a job. Entry-level jobs were put into five categories of physical demand ranging from light (lifting 20 pounds maximum with frequent lifts of 10 pounds) to very heavy (lifting in excess of 100 pounds with frequent lifts in excess of 50 pounds). Sixty-four percent of the jobs were deemed in the very heavy category, and although 42 percent of female soldiers were assigned to these positions, it was estimated that only 8 percent were physically qualified to accomplish the job tasks.[67] In contrast with the Air Force, which used the strength test to exclude personnel from heavy jobs, the Army employed MEPSCAT as a recruiting guidance tool and then eliminated it altogether in 1990.[68]

Finally, neither the Navy nor Marine Corps uses the PULHES profile to screen entrants, but the Marine Corps requires enlistees to pass a physical test, which for men involves three pullups, forty situps in 2 minutes or less, and a 1.5-mile run in 13 minutes or less. Women enlistees must do a 10-second flex-arm hang, seventeen situps in 1 minute or less, and a 0.75 mile run in 8.5 minutes or less.[69]

As long as appropriate physical standards, valid predictors of physical performance, and the means to measure them are still being developed, it is difficult to predict how effective women will be in combat jobs. What can be concluded, however, is that by most accepted measures men possess greater physical strength, on average, than women. The reasons for these dissimilarities remain controversial—is the more delicate construction natural or is it a product of a less active culture? But the structural and physiological differences between the sexes are well established. Differences in anthropometric characteristics and body composition— size, muscle mass, bone mass, fat distribution, and structure of the elbow

the Air Force, April 1992. Among a sample of more than 32,000 test takers, the Air Force reported that 68 percent of men and 0.8 percent of women met the 110-pound requirement. *Presidential Commission on Assignment of Women*, p. C-74.

67. Dennis M. Kowal, "Physical Capacity Screening for Job Selection and Classification: Technology for Bias?" in Nancy H. Loring, ed., *Women in the United States Armed Forces: Progress and Barriers in the 1980s* (Chicago: Inter-University Seminar on Armed Forces and Society, 1984), pp. 201–09. According to Carolyn Becraft, however, once the Army adopted a lower standard to accommodate 100 percent of the men, more than 30 percent of the women were able to meet it. Letter to the author, December 16, 1992.

68. *Presidential Commission on Assignment of Women*, p. C-13.

69. Briefing presented to the Presidential Commission on the Assignment of Women in the Armed Forces, Washington, D.C., April 6, 1992.

joints and pelvis—favor men in strength, explosive power, speed, and throwing and jumping (table 2-3).[70] Cardiorespiratory differences—size of heart and lungs, oxygen content, oxygen uptake (volume of oxygen that can be extracted from inspired air), average hemoglobin content, body temperature, and sweat gland function—give men an advantage in physical endurance and heat tolerance.

These physical differences are so clear that there are few sports at the amateur, much less professional, level in which both sexes compete. Even in segregated noncontact events, the application of different rules for men and women is widespread.

> In Olympic competition, for example, women jump a smaller hurdle at a shorter distance; they throw a lighter javelin, discus, and shot; they compete in different running events and in fewer jumping events; they compete in a heptathlon (seven events) instead of a decathlon (ten events); they compete in fewer and different gymnastic events; they skate and toboggan shorter distances; and, in every skiing event, they have less demanding requirements (in distance, vertical drop, total climb, or gates).[71]

The differences are also widely recognized in the armed forces. For example, to achieve a minimum satisfactory rating on the Navy's standard PT test, men are given two minutes to touch their toes 45 times and two minutes to complete at least 38 push-ups; women are required to complete 40 sit-ups and just 18 push-ups in the same time.[72]

In virtually all tests requiring physical prowess, the average man outperforms the average woman, but some women could be expected to meet minimum male standards and match or even exceed average male performance. It therefore follows that some women would possess the physical attributes that would render them more qualified than the average man for the most demanding tasks, perhaps including combat.[73]

70. The most obvious anthropometric differences are in height and weight: measurements taken in the late 1980s indicated that the mean height for Army men was 69.1 inches and for women 64.1 inches. The mean weights are 173.0 pounds and 136.7 pounds respectively. Claire C. Gordon and others, *1988 Anthropometric Survey of U.S. Army Personnel: Methods and Summary Statistics*, TR-89/044 (Natick, Mass.: U.S. Army Natick Research, Development and Engineering Center, September 1989), pp. 271, 321.

71. Mark J. Eitelberg, "Your Mother Wears Combat Boots . . . But Should She Pack a Gun?" Paper prepared for the ninety-eighth annual meeting of the American Psychological Association, August 1990, p. 18.

72. Data provided by Department of Defense, Office of the Assistant Secretary of Defense for Force Management and Personnel, April 1992.

73. In statistical terms, the physical attributes of men and women constitute two overlapping distributions with a significant difference between the means. The number of

Table 2-3. *Adult Anthropometric and Body-Composition Characteristics in Relation to Physical Performance, by Gender*

Characteristic	Men	Male advantage	Women	Female advantage
Height	Taller	Greater lung volume, speed, power	Shorter	Quick rotary
Weight	Heavier	Throwing power	. . .	. . .
Muscle mass of total body weight (percent)	Greater	Power, speed, strength	. . .	. . .
Body fat of total body weight (percent)	. . .	. . .	Greater	Buoyancy
Center of gravity	Higher	Rotary movement	Lower	Balance
Pelvis	Shallower, narrower, heavier	Running speed	. . .	. . .
Biiliac diameter (hips)	Narrower	Power production	Wider	Stability, childbirth
Biacromium diameter (shoulders)	Wider	Weight support production	Narrower	Flexibility
Chest girth	Greater	Thoracic cavity ventilation capacity	. . .	. . .
Trunk length	. . .	. . .	Relatively longer	Lower center of gravity
Leg length	Relatively longer	Acceleration, speed, power, greater kicking velocity	Relatively shorter	Agility
Elbow joint	Arms parallel from shoulders[a]	Leverage in throwing supporting weight	. . .	. . .

Source: James A. Peterson and others, "Summary Report on Project 60: A Comparison of Two Types of Physical Training Programs in the Performance of 16- to 18-Year-Old Women," U.S. Military Academy, May 3, 1976, pp. 119–20. The same terminology is used in this table as in the source; some detail has been omitted.

[a] As opposed to women, whose arms form an X from shoulders.

Should these women, then, be denied the opportunity to serve in those specialties?

One common male opinion was echoed in 1976 by General William C. Westmoreland, former Army chief of staff, in a news conference opposing the entrance of women to the nation's military academies. "Maybe you could find one woman in 10,000 who could lead in combat, but she would be a freak and we're not running the military academy for freaks. . . . The pendulum has gone too far. . . . They're asking women to do impossible things. I don't believe women can carry a pack, live in a foxhole or go a week without taking a bath."[74] Retired Brigadier General Elizabeth P. Hoisington, a former director of the Women's Army Corps concurred: "In my whole lifetime I have never known ten women whom I thought could endure three months under actual combat conditions."[75]

Even one of the strongest and most articulate voices for military women, retired Air Force Major General Jeanne Holm, stopped short of recommending ground combat jobs be opened for women. During congressional testimony she said, "women could fly combat jets, serve on combat ships, fire missiles and artillery, and do any job that requires skill rather than muscle. . . . I have great difficulty with ground combat where the number one concern is physical strength."[76]

But others question the justification for excluding *all* women based on a law of averages:

> Why are women treated as a group rather than as individuals (the same way men are treated)? . . . It shouldn't really have much to do with individual qualifications, because the armed forces have long maintained that "qualified soldiers make good soldiers because they are qualified." If women can qualify for combat assignment as *individuals*, what is the purpose of examining group averages or comparing the average abilities of women with men? Is there something inherently common to all women that should make each and every woman unfit for combat duty?[77]

---

women who would be expected to meet a given male standard, then, would depend on the extent of the overlap, which varies according to the physical demands involved. Although the parameters of these distributions have not been developed for all physical activities found in the armed forces, some results can be found in *Presidential Commission on Assignment of Women*, p. C-8.

74. "General Says Women 'Silly' at West Point," *Washington Post*, May 30, 1976, p. A15.
75. Quoted in Holm, *Women in the Military*, p. 342.
76. Holm, *Women in the Military*, p. 339.
77. Eitelberg, "Your Mother Wears Combat Boots," p. 23.

Another perspective was provided by an Israeli military historian in testimony before the Presidential Commission on the Assignment of Women.

> Are there some women capable of doing it? Undoubtedly. Are most women [physically] less capable of doing it than most men? Undoubtedly. And that is the best possible reason for excluding women from combat . . . the added overhead that you would need in order to incorporate those females would be so large as to make the whole exercise counterproductive.[78]

The small number of women who would be expected to meet the physical demands of ground combat duty was also acknowledged by Carolyn Becraft, one of the major activists in the crusade to remove combat restrictions: "Most women would not meet the infantry standard . . . and [the services] could justify closing [the infantry] completely to women if only 5 percent could do it. That would be OK, as long as the job is based on gender-neutral physical and mental standards."[79]

Devising gender-neutral physical standards, however, would encounter significant obstacles and arouse serious controversy. Although there is a gathering consensus that a single standard should be established, there is less agreement on what the standard should be. Many would argue that women should be held to the same physical standards as men for entrance into various training programs and in physical fitness tests. If so, few would qualify, and most would be unable to pass the parts of the fitness test (for example, push-ups) that depend on upper body strength. Others would contend, however, that because much about the relation between standards and job performance is not understood, there would be a tendency to set standards arbitrarily high. A realistic middle ground has been suggested by a Navy physiologist, that would recognize the difference between physical strength requirements and fitness standards.[80]

The question of physical standards goes to the heart of a controversy that involves weighing two powerful imperatives, equal opportunity and

78. Testimony of Martin Van Crevald reported in David Evans, "Officer's Training School Should Test Women's True Mettle," *Chicago Tribune*, August 14, 1992, p. 17. Van Crevald, a strong critic of women in combat, contended that "the very fact that this issue is being discussed . . . simply shows that you [the United States] don't take the military seriously."

79. Quoted in Grant Willis, "Strength May Settle Combat Issue," *Army Times*, July 13, 1992, p. 21.

80. Willis, "Strength May Settle Combat Issue," p. 21.

national security. Prohibiting women who meet appropriate physical standards from competing for an entire class of jobs conflicts with the essence of equal opportunity, which attaches rights to people judged solely on their merits. But just how far the armed forces should be expected to go to accommodate equal opportunity principles to the potential detriment of military readiness is an open question.

EMOTIONAL SUITABILITY. In a society that traditionally has shielded its women from the brutality of combat, people cannot imagine exposing them to battlefield conditions, here vividly described by a seasoned combat veteran:

> I know from experience in three combat tours that the combat environment is an ugly one. For the ground soldier it is characterized by loneliness and desolation, weary marches, at times relentless heat, bitter cold, torrential rains, filth, pestilence, disease, the slime of dripping dugouts, and the stench of human carnage. These are coupled with feelings of depression that stem from fear, uncertainty and long separation from loved ones. The situation calls for an antic toughness that women do not normally have.[81]

It is often argued that because of innate differences in temperament between the sexes, women are not likely to function effectively in such situations. Today's feminists bristle at such assertions, yet the masculinity-femininity test, the Rorschach ink blot tests, and other devices have confirmed typical differences in personality.

> In word association, females tend to choose words for articles of dress, personal adornment, colors, aesthetic appraisal, domestic things and happenings, and words indicating a "kind" and "sympathetic" social orientation. Conversely, the male preference is for words describing outdoor phenomena, activity and adventure, science and machinery, political, business and commercial enterprise. . . . the key masculine quality is "the aggressive, adventurous, enterprising, outwardly directed disposition: the tendency to pugnacity and self-assertiveness." The outstanding feminine traits are "the actively sympathetic, the inwardly directed disposition: the maternal impulse and the tender feelings, concern with domestic affairs.[82]

Such descriptions, of course, have become highly controversial. Many feminists dismiss them as anachronistic stereotypes. Yet the public's image of gender personality differences persists. When asked to identify the characteristics associated with either men or women, respondents to a nationwide Gallup survey most often described men as aggressive,

81. Andrew J. Gatsis, "Women Can't Be Warriors," *Raleigh News and Observer*, August 26, 1992, p. 11.

82. Ann Oakley, *Sex, Gender, and Society* (Harper and Row, 1972), pp. 49–50.

strong, proud, disorganized, courageous, confident, and independent, and women as emotional, talkative, sensitive, affectionate, patient, romantic, and moody.[83] Although most observers agree that men are more aggressive than women, there is less agreement about the etiology: are the differences cultural or biological?[84]

In any event, personality differences led Margaret Mead, one of the most widely respected anthropologists of her day, to conclude that "the historical and comparative material at least suggests that it may be highly undesirable to permit women, trained to inhibit aggressive behavior, to take part in offensive warfare. Defensive warfare, on the other hand, does not have the same disadvantages, as it invokes the biological basis of defense of the nest and the young."[85]

Here again, however, discussion has focused on the average woman rather than individual women. As in the case of physical attributes, some women would be emotionally suited for combat. For example, women played a conspicuous role in many terrorist organizations that arose in the 1970s, including the Symbionese Liberation Army, the Popular Front for the Liberation of Palestine, the Croatian Nationalists, and the Baader-Meinhof gang. The numbers of such women, however, have been small.

APTITUDE. Closely related to the suitability of a woman's personality for combat is the question of aptitude. All prospective volunteers are administered the Armed Services Vocational Aptitude Battery (ASVAB), one of the principal instruments used to determine general military trainability. The test battery includes subtests that are combined

83. "Unlike 1975, Today Most Americans Think Men Have It Better," *Gallup Poll Monthly* (February 1990), pp. 25–36.

84. According to the February 1990 Gallup survey, 44 percent of women and 35 percent of men felt that the differences were a result of upbringing, while 49 percent of men and 40 percent of women felt that they were biological. "Unlike 1975 . . . Men Have It Better," pp. 30, 36.

85. Margaret Mead, "A National Service System as a Solution to a Variety of National Problems," in Sol Tax, ed., *The Draft: A Handbook of Facts and Alternatives* (University of Chicago Press, 1967), p. 108. This thesis is supported by the experience of women in the Israeli army. In the first phase of the War of Liberation in 1948, women, who constituted 15 percent of the soldiers in the Haganah, reportedly "shared in both the active and defensive battle activities." When fighting resumed in July 1948 after the aborted United Nations truce, the Israeli Army captured the initiative in a series of offensive operations. With a change in tactics and organization, "there were fewer battle tasks for women to perform," and a noncombat role for Israeli women was institutionalized in the postwar army. Lionel Tiger and Joseph Shepher, *Women in the Kibbutz* (Harcourt Brace Jovanovich, 1975), p. 186.

Table 2-4. *Means and Standard Deviations of Percentile Scores of 18- to 23-Year-Olds on Armed Services Vocational Aptitude Battery (ASVAB) Subtests, by Gender, 1980*

	Mean		Standard deviation	
Subtests	Men	Women	Men	Women
Difference favors men				
General science	51.3	47.9	10.1	8.9
Arithmetic reasoning	51.7	48.9	10.5	9.8
Auto and shop information	51.4	40.9	9.8	6.8
Mathematics knowledge	52.6	51.1	11.1	10.3
Mechanical comprehension	51.2	43.9	9.7	7.8
Electronics information	51.5	44.3	9.9	8.5
Difference favors women				
Paragraph comprehension	50.6	52.4	10.0	9.2
Numerical operations	47.6	49.6	10.8	10.4
Coding speed	49.9	54.1	9.8	10.0
No difference				
Word knowledge	50.8	50.9	10.3	9.8

Source: Office of the Assistant Secretary of Defense for Manpower, Reserve Affairs, and Logistics, *Profile of American Youth: 1980 Nationwide Administration of the Armed Services Vocational Aptitude Battery* (Department of Defense, March 1982), p. 90.

to form composites used to determine eligibility for specific training courses. Entrance into Army infantry training, for instance, requires a certain minimum score on the combat composite consisting of four subtests: arithmetic reasoning, coding speed, auto and shop information, and mechanical comprehension. As table 2-4 shows, men more often meet the requirements because they tend to outscore women on all subtests except coding speed. The results of a nationwide administration of the test in 1980 suggest that 72 percent of American men 17 to 23 years old could be expected to qualify for infantry training compared with 62 percent of women.[86]

This difference is not as formidable as the physical and emotional differences. Besides, although aptitude test scores are considered reasonable predictors of training success, their validity as predictors of performance remains under active study.

IMPLICATIONS FOR UNIT COHESION. One of the most controversial questions involved in the wrangling over allowing women in combat, however, is the effect they would have on group performance, or in the case of combat groups, small unit cohesion. But an understanding of the behav-

86. Eitelberg, *Manpower for Military Occupations*, p. 214.

ior and performance of men in groups, particularly under combat conditions, is far from complete. An understanding of the behavior and performance of women under these conditions is scant. And very little is known about the effects of combining men and women.[87] And given the ambiguities involved with defining—much less measuring—cohesion, there is almost no empirical basis for drawing conclusions.

Nonetheless, the term *combat* has been virtually synonymous with male bonding in social groups from which women are excluded.[88] Male bonding has been particularly crucial, it is argued, in groups involved in confronting disruptions of social order, such as occur in politics, war, and police matters. The hypothesis implies that in matters pertaining to organized aggression "not only will males and females reject other females as potential leaders and defenders, but that males will reject females as colleagues."[89]

Studies in the social psychology of combat personnel have supported a strong connection between the concept of masculinity and fighting prowess. The most respected research on the combat soldier during World War II concluded that the most general code by which members of combat units were judged was "Be a man." The core conceptions of masculinity included "courage, endurance and toughness, lack of squeamishness when confronted with shocking or distasteful stimuli, avoidance of display of weakness in general, reticence about emotional or idealistic matters, and sexual competency."[90] How a soldier behaved under combat conditions was recognized as a test of his manhood. The combat fraternity enjoyed wide respect, and their locker room etiquette was taken for granted. "Combat people are an exclusive set," wrote Bill Mauldin, "and if they want to be that way, it is their privilege."[91]

---

87. For a discussion of theories of combat behavior, the primary work is Samuel A. Stouffer and others, *The American Soldier: Combat and Its Aftermath*, vol. 2 (Princeton University Press, 1949). For more contemporary treatments, see William Darryl Henderson, *Cohesion: The Human Element In Combat* (Washington: National Defense University Press, 1985); and Charles G. Moskos, Jr., *The American Enlisted Man: The Rank and File in Today's Military* (Russell Sage Foundation, 1970).

88. One of the principal proponents of male bonding, anthropologist Lionel Tiger, suggested that "there is a biological program that results in a 'bonding' between males which is important for politics as the program of male-female bonding is for reproduction." See Lionel Tiger, "Male Dominance? Yes, Alas. A Sexist Plot? No," *New York Times Magazine* (October 25, 1970), p. 132.

89. Lionel Tiger, *Men in Groups* (London: Thomas Nelson, 1969), p. 85.

90. Stouffer and others, *The American Soldier*, vol. 2, p. 131.

91. Bill Mauldin, *Up Front* (Henry Holt, 1945), p. 58.

The close link between masculinity and combat performance was also verified in a study of combat experience during the Korean conflict. It found that soldiers who had been identified as effective fighters by their peers in units that had seen combat tended to "be more masculine" than nonfighters. "Masculinity appears to be a fairly clear-cut area" differentiating fighters from nonfighters, the study group concluded. "Both masculinity of interests as reflected in the Strong Vocational patterns and masculinity-femininity scales of the personality measures differentiated the two groups."[92]

In support of that view, Charles Moskos contends that one of the only ways to convince men in combat to do "an essentially irrational thing— put themselves in a position where they are likely to get killed"—is to appeal to their masculinity. Warning that there can be no "androgenous military," Moskos points out that the idea that fighting is a masculine trait predates any written history and could well be genetic.[93]

Many feminists would consider such views anachronisms and indicative of continuing prejudice, but other observers contend that it would be risky to change the masculine ethos of ground combat groups. According to David Marlowe, chief of military psychiatry at the Walter Reed Army Institute of Research,

> In the world of the combat soldier . . . masculinity is an essential measure of capability. In an interaction between male bonding and widespread cultural norms, the maleness of an act is the measure of its worth and thus a measure of one's ability. While many may disapprove of these norms, they have been and are, as a matter of ethnographic fact, the operative ones in much of military society and particularly in the combat group.

"If we are serious about the missions that are mandated for the combat arms," Marlowe concluded, "we cannot afford to make them a locus of social experimentation. The reason is simple: we can afford to do nothing that would lessen their combat potential and power, else we run the risk of losing the war and sacrificing a force that was not the best structured to perform its job."[94]

92. Robert L. Egbert and others, *Fighter I: An Analysis of Combat Fighters and Non-Fighters*, technical report 44 (Presidio of Monterey, Calif.: U.S. Army Leadership Human Research Unit, December 1957), p. 26. See also p. iii.

93. William Matthews, "Military Has Basic Link to Sex," *Army Times*, July 27, 1992, p. 16.

94. David H. Marlowe, "The Manning of the Force and the Structure of Battle: Part 2—Men and Women," in Robert K. Fullinwider, *Conscripts and Volunteers: Military Requirements, Social Justice, and the All-Volunteer Force* (Rowman and Allanheld, 1983), pp. 194, 195.

The importance of male bonding and unit cohesion is, however, viewed differently by the various types of combat units and thus by the individual services. Male bonding is perhaps most prominent among ground combat units, where interdependence is most crucial. It lessens in importance in air and naval combat activities that depend more on individual performance or are inherently less dangerous.[95] These differences were evident in the results of surveys conducted by the Roper organization in 1992 under the auspices of the Presidential Commission on the Assignment of Women in the Armed Forces (Herres commission). Overall, 56 percent of military respondents supported current policies that restrict women from assignment to combat duties. But when the results were categorized by type of combat duty, 30 percent opposed the assignment of women to combat aircraft, 29 percent were against opening combat ships to women, and 49 percent opposed women's holding ground combat jobs (Army and Marine Corps personnel opposed women in ground combat by 56 and 75 percent, respectively). Moreover, most of those who favored assigning women to combat specialties felt that they should be given the assignments only if they volunteer.[96]

Service members responding to the survey were especially concerned about women's effect on unit cohesion. Forty-one percent said that assigning women to direct combat positions would block cohesion or bonding. The strongest responses again came from Army and Marine Corps personnel (49 percent and 64 percent, respectively). Those serving in combat roles were more likely than those in support specialties (63 percent to 37 percent) to hold that view.[97]

OTHER CONCERNS. Other concerns have been expressed by those fearful that introducing women would impair the effectiveness of combat units.

95. This is a contentious point. Many aviators, for example, would argue that male cohesion is just as important in air combat. For example, twenty-one of twenty-three Navy Top Gun instructor pilots supported the view presented to the President's Commission on the Assignment of Women: "When you are out there in your fleet squadron, it is very important that you act as one . . . you have to act as a unit. . . . We don't believe you can act as a unit unless you keep it the way it is, where it's the bonding—it's that intangible, the bonding, that makes a squadron good, better, and we don't believe you can have that go on if we have females in aviation." *Presidential Commission on Assignment of Women*, p. 71.

96. "Attitudes Regarding the Assignment of Women in the Armed Forces: The Military Perspective," survey conducted for the Presidential Commission on the Assignment of Women in the Armed Forces (Roper Organization, September 1992), pp. 45–55.

97. "Attitudes Regarding Assignment of Women . . . Military Perspective," pp. 35, 39.

The presence of women will affect the types of men who volunteer. Military organizations, it is argued, particularly ranger, airborne, and other elite combat units often attract men because of their machismo image. Introducing women into such units could undermine that attraction, as one high-ranking Navy official suggested during congressional testimony in 1975 on the admission of women to the nation's military academies.

> Since the inception of the Continental Navy, later the U.S. Navy, traditional male domination of warfare and seafaring has continued. Only recently has there been pressure for change. The naval profession—specifically the business of going to sea—has been advertised as, and accepted as, a closed club for men.
>
> The present male-dominated, sea-going facet of Navy life is one that is understood and accepted by the country and the men in the Navy. Men join the Navy for many different reasons; however, a certain portion join and remain in the Navy because they enjoy being in a job which has been historically associated with fellowship among men in a difficult and dangerous endeavor. Changing the fabric of the Navy by integrating women into all combat roles might well reduce the attractions of the Navy to this segment of mankind, as well as to some of those men who might, in the future, join the Navy and make it a career.[98]

This attitude appeared to prevail at the Naval Academy ten years after integration. In 1987 Navy researchers found "a persistent belief [among male midshipmen] that women do not belong at the Naval Academy. Some of the men resent women perhaps for debasing the masculine mystique long associated with the Naval Academy."[99]

Because women have not served in combat units, however, there is no direct evidence that their introduction would dissuade men with strong masculine characteristics from serving in those units. The limited research on the subject yields conflicting results. David Marlowe found, for example, that when women were being integrated into Army basic training units in the late 1970s, men in coed units, unlike those in all-male units, "had judged *themselves* wanting. If women could do all the things they could do, how good could they [the men] be? The answer of

98. Testimony of Admiral Worth Bagley, then Vice Chief of Naval Operations, *Hearings on H.R. 9832 to Eliminate Discrimination Based on Sex with Respect to the Appointment and Admission of Persons to the Service Academies*, Hearings before the House Armed Services Committee, 93 Cong. 2 sess. (GPO, 1975), p. 120.

99. "The Integration of Women into the Brigade of Midshipmen," report to the superintendent submitted by the Women Midshipmen Study Group (United States Naval Academy, November 1987), p. 88.

most was, 'not very good.' "[100] By implication, then, the presence of women in combat units would degrade men's self-image and self-esteem, which is based largely on their masculinity.

Studies of changes in the sex-role traits of male and female cadets at the Army and Air Force academies, however, suggest that the coed environment is not an emasculating experience. Surveys at both institutions in the early 1980s revealed that male cadets believed their masculine traits had strengthened and their female traits had weakened during their academy experience.[101]

Another perspective was provided in the 1992 Roper survey, in which 18 percent of male respondents said the assignment of women to combat would decrease the likelihood that they would remain in the armed forces. Not surprisingly, the proportions were much larger among Army and Marine Corps personnel (25 and 39 percent, respectively) and among those serving in combat specialties (33 percent).[102]

The presence of women in combat units will foster fraternization and sexual entanglements. A good deal of concern has been expressed that fraternization would impair military discipline and effectiveness. Social alliances and sexual pairings, which are inevitable in any organization, are also believed to weaken authority and morale within the unit. The situation is all the more damaging when interpersonal relationships occur between service members of different ranks, because the appearance of partiality can compromise the military chain of command.

Although successive generations have become more accommodating in their views of the roles of women in all aspects of American society, the military services have continued to struggle with problems of fraternization, sexual harassment, and sex discrimination, especially where women have made inroads into nontraditional occupations and settings. In recent years the Navy has seemed particularly vulnerable to these charges, prompting an internal study directed by the secretary of the

100. Marlowe, "Manning of the Force," p. 194.

101. Lois B. DeFleur and Rebecca L. Warner, "The Impact of Military Service on Women's Status: A Neglected Area of Inquiry," in Nancy H. Loring, ed., *Women in the United States Armed Forces: Progress and Barriers in the 1980s* (Chicago: Inter-University Seminar on Armed Forces and Society, 1984), p. 10. It is interesting to note the differences between the perceptions of women at the two institutions. Women cadets at West Point, like their male counterparts, perceived a growth in masculine traits and a decrease in feminine traits, but those at the Air Force Academy saw a growth in their feminine characteristics and no change in their masculine characteristics.

102. "Attitudes Regarding Assignment of Women . . . Military Perspective," p. 77.

Navy in 1987 that recommended the service provide a clearer policy on fraternization and improve training on proper interpersonal relationships.[103]

These initiatives will likely have little immediate effect, given that such behavior is deeply entrenched in male culture and even "enlightened" men find it difficult to break with stereotypes. Ambivalence toward the proximity of women in the military was evident in the views of one naval aviator quoted in the *Los Angeles Times*:

> The aviator said he "logically" felt "at ease" with women in the military performing equal tasks—even combat missions, alongside men. "But my gut tells me something else. There's this all-encompassing sexual tension loose in society that is simply out of place in some military settings." Putting women in positions where they could be an amorous distraction to men, he said, "could affect your concentration. It could affect a fellow pilot or the guy who fixes your plane. It could kill you."[104]

These sexual issues were thrust into the national limelight after the incident at the Tailhook Convention in September 1991, when a number of male naval aviators were accused of sexual assault and harassment by a group of women, including some fellow naval aviators.[105] The incident was later offered as evidence by those on both sides of the women-in-combat question to support their case.

Those in favor of maintaining restrictions contended that such situations could be expected to occur when women venture into male preserves. Those favoring combat roles for women argued that the Tailhook incident was a manifestation of the prevailing attitude of male warriors: a disrespect for military perpetuated by women's second-class noncombatant status and male expectations of their substandard performance. As a female naval aviator explained, "All of my 20 years . . . in this business tells me that if you cannot share the equal risks and hazards in arduous duty, then you are not equal. . . . And if the institution can discriminate against you, then it's not a big leap for . . . bigots to decide that 'Well, I can harass you and I can get away with it.' "[106]

103. Chief of Naval Operations, *Navy Study Group's Report on Progress of Women in the Navy* (Department of the Navy, December 5, 1987), pp. 4-5, 4-6.
104. Melissa Healy and James Bornemeier, "For Women in the Navy, Rough Waters Run Deep," *Los Angeles Times*, June 28, 1992, p. 1.
105. For a description of the Tailhook incident and its implications, see *Women in the Military: The Tailhook Affair and the Problem of Sexual Harassment*, report of the Military Personnel and Compensation Subcommittee and Defense Policy Panel, House Armed Services Committee, 102 Cong. 2 sess. (GPO, 1992)
106. "Women and Stone Age Warriors," *New York Times*, July 8, 1992, p. A18.

Observers also need to consider the consequences for unit performance of the sexual situations that would arise from introducing relatively small numbers of women into the close proximity and spartan conditions of the combat unit field environment. Speculating on the effect of introducing women into the Navy's elite SEAL units, Rear Admiral Raymond Smith, head of the Naval Special Warfare Command, commented,

> I recognize that a woman might not have any interest in developing a personal relationship, but my experience in life tells me that men, being what we are, will in fact complicate this issue. Sex in males is the most powerful drive at a young age, and whether, in a given situation, a man or a woman initiates the relationship is irrelevant. All that is relevant is that it will happen, and when it does, it will create within a SEAL platoon a distraction, at best, and a romantic or fraternizing situation, at worst, but ultimately male and female personal relationships will reduce our combat effectiveness.[107]

The Persian Gulf experience might have been expected to provide useful data about sexual relationships within military units in wartime, but virtually no information was released by the armed forces. In 1992, however, in a Roper poll of military personnel who had served in the conflict, 64 percent said they knew of sexual activity within their integrated units. Of these respondents, 55 percent believed the activity had harmed morale and 36 percent believed it had degraded unit readiness.[108]

The Navy, meanwhile, acknowledged that twenty-nine women, 8 percent of the female crew on the destroyer tender *Acadia*, had become pregnant while on an eight-month deployment to the Persian Gulf. Navy officials deplored the unusual media attention, pointing out that this pregnancy rate was in line with their normal peacetime experience (8.9 percent) and that most of the pregnancies began before deployment.[109]

---

107. *Presidential Commission on Assignment of Women*, p. 77. The Naval Academy is not a combat environment (though plebes might disagree), but sexual relationships did not escape scrutiny in a study of integration there: "putting 4,000 young men, at the peak of their sexual development, into a single large dormitory, depriving them of normal social contact for days or weeks at a time, then throwing 400 young women into their midst is bound to lead to trouble." See "Integration of Women into the Brigade of Midshipmen," p. 89.

108. "Attitudes Regarding the Assignment of Women . . . Military Perspective," pp. 120–23.

109. Data provided by Carolyn Becraft, December 1992.

The Navy found the media's dubbing of the *Acadia* as "the love boat" especially offensive, claiming that it "detracted from the brilliant performance of women in the gulf."[110]

Men will resent special treatment accorded woman counterparts. One of the most frequent complaints by men in integrated units has been the existence of a double standard, either in gender-normed physical requirements or in more lenient treatment of women by superiors. Although this phenomenon is believed widespread, there is little evidence to support hard conclusions. One of the more obvious bones of contention, however, has been the gender-based standards applied to mandatory physical fitness testing conducted by each of the armed services.

Many men also resent having to take up the slack when women in their units are unable to carry their load, both figuratively and literally. These charges were especially prevalent during the early years of the expansion as women were assigned to demanding nontraditional occupations for which physical standards had not been established. In the mid-1970s, for example, many Air Force women assigned to aircraft maintenance duties reported they were not strong enough to change aircraft tires and brakes, remove batteries and crew seats, close drag chute doors, break torque on bolts, and lift heavy stands. Most female Marine telephone repairers were unable to climb poles while hoisting the necessary equipment, which weighed 50 pounds. And supervisors of Navy women serving as boatswains' mates on naval vessels said "women cannot physically do much of the work, which includes lifting and handling sandbags that weigh 100 pounds, paint cans that weigh from 72 to 94 pounds, and boat lines that weigh as much as 7 pounds a foot."[111]

The assignment restrictions that apply to pregnant women are also resented as preferential treatment by some men. The Navy reported, for example, a deterioration in morale because of the perception that "some junior enlisted women become pregnant primarily to get out of sea duty or an unpleasant situation."[112] Sixty percent of Roper survey respondents who had served in integrated units during the Persian Gulf conflict said "women in their unit did get pregnant prior to or while deployed in the

110. Jon Nordheimer, "Women's Role in Combat: The War Resumes," *New York Times*, May 26, 1991, p. 1.
111. Comptroller General of the United States, *Job Opportunities for Women in the Military: Progress and Problems* (1976), pp. 13–27.
112. Nordheimer, "Women's Role in Combat."

Persian Gulf." Among those respondents 46 percent believed the pregnancies had impaired readiness, and 59 percent indicated that they
harmed unit morale.[113]

The services have generally been able to deal with the pregnancies,
which have been limited to support units. But whether the problem would
be as manageable in a combat unit, which demands far more teamwork
and burden sharing, remains to be seen. If women were assigned to
combat units, the issue could be circumvented, of course, by immediately
transferring those who become pregnant.[114] This could intensify the re-
sentment among their male colleagues, however, if they thought women
chose pregnancy as a way to avoid serving in a combat unit. In any event,
this policy would increase personnel turnover and exact a penalty on unit
morale and readiness.

EXTENT OF INTEGRATION. The severity of many of the problems I have
discussed could turn on the extent to which women are integrated into
combat units. Research suggests that the performance of mixed-sex
groups is sensitive to the composition of the mix. As long as women
remain a small minority, men tend to view them according to stereotypes
and fulfill their own need to project the male image. When this happens,
women tend to be isolated, the male group remains in conflict with them,
and group productivity suffers.[115]

---

113. "Attitudes Regarding the Assignment of Women . . . Military Perspective,"
pp. 118–19.
114. The prospect of pregnant women in combat units prompted a bizarre exchange
between two strong-minded adversaries during congressional hearings on the integration
of women into the military academies. According to Congressman Lawrence P. McDonald
of Georgia:
    It is truly difficult to visualize an effective defense force that included a portion of
    officers serving while 7, 8, or 9 months pregnant. Going on, can anyone seriously
    imagine an officer giving a lecture or leading a tank column but requiring a pause to
    breast-feed her infant? That situation, which might produce a box office triumph in a
    broadway comedy, has no serious parallel in the real world.
Congresswoman Bella S. Abzug of New York responded:
    women were lactating on the frontier of this Nation; and women were lactating on the
    frontiers of Israel when they fought to establish that homeland. They were lactating
    during wars throughout the history of this great Nation and the history of the world.
    Somehow or other that did not stop progress.
Congressional Record, daily ed., May 20, 1975, pp. 15454, 15455.
115. For example, see Ross A. Webber, "Perceptions and Behaviors in Mixed Sex Work
Teams," Industrial Relations, vol. 15 (May 1976); and Diane N. Ruble and E. Tory Higgins,
"Effects of Group Sex Composition on Self-Presentation and Sex Typing," Journal of Social
Issues, vol.32, no.3 (1976), pp. 125–32.

Studies of the integration experience at Yale and Princeton Universities, for example, found that social problems were more common when women constituted 25 percent or less of the student population. Some tended to become superwomen and to make more male friends than they normally would, while men tended to reject them socially as inferior.[116]

Similarly, in a study of American corporations, Rosabeth Moss Kanter identified the problems confronted when women are tokens in "skewed" groups, that is, when they are outnumbered by men by at least five to one. "As long as numbers are low," Kanter contended, organizations considered disruptions of interaction around tokens as "a huge deflection from [their] central purposes, a drain of energy, leading to the conclusion that it is not worth having people like tokens around."[117] If these situations are disruptive in the American civilian workplace, they would be all the more challenging in a combat setting in which the dominant group has placed a premium on masculinity.

Thus the number of women who would be interested in filling combat positions is important. In the 1992 Roper survey, 46 percent of military women respondents indicated that they would be "likely" to volunteer for direct combat assignments.[118] Wide differences in response could be expected by women from the different services, but the number in the sample was too small to yield statistically reliable results by service. An independent survey of Army personnel, however, reported that only 12 percent of enlisted women, 10 percent of female noncommissioned officers, and 14 percent of female officers would volunteer for combat duty.[119]

Public Opinion

American society has traditionally sought to protect American women from the risks of capture or death in combat. But the arguments to maintain the status quo have become less persuasive as equal opportunity

116. James H. Thomas and Dirk C. Prather, "Integration of Females into a Previously All-Male Institution," in *Proceedings of the Fifth Symposium on Psychology in the Air Force* (U.S. Air Force Academy, Department of Behavioral Sciences and Leadership, April 1976), pp. 100–01.

117. Rosabeth Moss Kanter, *Men and Women of the Corporation* (Basic Books, 1977), p. 239.

118. "Attitudes Regarding Assignment of Women . . . Military Perspective," p. 84.

119. Laura L. Miller and Charles Moskos, "1992 Survey on Gender in the Military," unpublished tabulations, August 28, 1992, table 5.

for women has become a national goal and as modern weapons and tactics of war have narrowed the distinction between combat and noncombat duties.

New trends in public perception are evident, for example, in Gallup surveys during the 1980s that sought to gauge public opinion related to women and the military. In a 1979 poll, 43 percent of respondents had said women should be included in a future draft, but less than 20 percent approved of women in combat jobs. In a similar 1980 poll, nearly 50 percent favored conscription of women and 22 percent approved of women in combat jobs.[120] In another poll of 18- to 24-year-olds, 61 percent of the men said women should be drafted if a draft became necessary, but only 39 percent of the women agreed. Two of three respondents said women should serve in combat, but *only if they volunteered*.[121] In a 1981 Gallup poll conducted soon after the Supreme Court decided women could be excluded from draft registration, 60 percent of respondents agreed with the decision.[122]

In 1982 the National Opinion Research Center, affiliated with the University of Chicago, undertook an extensive survey of national attitudes toward minorities and women in the armed forces. Eighty percent of respondents supported maintaining or increasing the number of women in the military, and an equal proportion believed women should be assigned to nontraditional combat-support jobs. A surprisingly large share supported women as jet fighter pilots (62 percent), missile gunners (59 percent), and crewmembers on combat ships (57 percent). About 34 percent approved of women being involved in hand-to-hand combat, a finding that the authors considered "astounding because it is so high, not because it is low."[123]

The degree to which poll results are sensitive not only to the context and the structure of the questions but to current events was demonstrated in January 1990, shortly after news accounts of the exploits of Captain

120. George H. Gallup, *The Gallup Poll, Public Opinion 1979* (Wilmington, Del.: Scholarly Resources, 1980), pp. 150–53; and *The Gallup Poll, Public Opinion 1980* (Wilmington, Del.: Scholarly Resources, 1981), pp. 146–49.

121. Holm, *Women in the Military*, pp. 352–53.

122. George H. Gallup, *The Gallup Poll, Public Opinion 1981* (Wilmington, Del.: Scholarly Resources, 1982), pp. 182–83.

123. James A. Davis, Jennifer Lauby, and Paul B. Sheatsley, *Americans View the Military: Public Opinion in 1982*, report 131 (National Opinion Research Center, University of Chicago, April 1983), pp. 32–35.

Linda Bray during the U.S. invasion on Panama. When a *New York Times*/CBS survey asked, "Do you think women members of the armed forces should be allowed to serve in combat units if they want to, or don't you think so?" 72 percent of respondents answered yes.[124] How much this response might have been influenced by the Bray episode or by the wording of the question is unclear, but one scholar has commented that the qualification " 'if they want to' turned a matter of military effectiveness into one of fairness or free choice . . . different wording would have elicited a different response."[125]

The Roper poll conducted in July 1992 for the Herres commission, also indicated public support for women in combat, especially if the assignments are voluntary. Support varied according to the specific duties involved. One-half to two-thirds of respondents favored women as crew members on combat aircraft, ships, and tanks, but 57 percent also favored keeping the jobs of infantry soldiers closed to women and 52 percent said they should not be allowed to join Marines engaged in amphibious operations.[126]

The limitations of surveys trying to measure in peacetime the feelings the American public might have in wartime were illustrated early in the Persian Gulf crisis. The public became concerned that mothers were being deployed to a potential combat zone. That some women were single parents, others had military spouses who were also slated for deployment, and some had infant children captured the attention of the nation, thanks in large part to the news media's fascination with "war orphans." *People* magazine featured a cover with the caption "Mom Goes to War," depicting an Air Force woman clutching her eleven-month-old daughter. The scene was described in the accompanying article: "With tears and brave smiles, Air Force pilot Joy Johnson and thousands of American mothers are saying goodbye to their families to face unknown dangers in

124. Elaine Sciolino, "Can Mother Fill Combat Boots Well?" *San Diego Union*, February 11, 1990, p. D6.

125. Eitelberg, "Your Mother Wears Combat Boots," p. 13.

126. "Attitudes Regarding the Assignment of Women in the Armed Forces: The Public Perspective," survey conducted for the Presidential Commission on the Assignment of Women in the Armed Forces (Roper Organization, August 1992), p. 55. The limitations inherent in such polling were illustrated in the inconsistencies of the responses. For example, respondents were evenly split when the choice was whether current policies on women in combat should be changed, with opinions shifting markedly as other options were presented. A large number of respondents, moreover, were uninformed on the issue, believing that women were already serving in combat positions, including in the infantry.

the Gulf." A ten-year-old child's question punctuated the drama of the situation: "Mommy, what if you die?"[127]

In a February 1991 Associated Press poll, two out of every three respondents agreed that it was "unacceptable for the United States to send women with young children to the war zone."[128] Surprised that the armed forces would deploy mothers to a war zone, Representative Beverly Byron sponsored legislation to prohibit the reassignment of an active-duty parent or the mobilization of a reservist who has a child six months of age or younger.[129] The proposal cleared the House but was killed in conference when Ohio Senator John Glenn, chairman of the Senate Armed Services Subcommittee on Personnel, opposed the legislation so as not to set a precedent. Instead he proposed a compromise calling for the Pentagon to adopt uniform assignment policies and to establish clear procedures to consider exemptions case by case.[130]

Sensing that the opposition to her original proposal was incurred mostly by its inclusion of male parents, Byron resubmitted her proposal modified to include only female military personnel. As a result the military services have adopted uniform policies with regard to single parents, military couples, and mothers of young children. No exemptions are granted based solely on marital or parental status, but all mothers are exempt for four months after giving birth from assignment to a location that is dependent restricted. Likewise, single parents and one member of a military couple are exempt for four months following the adoption of a child.[131]

The single-parent issue attracted more attention than it deserved. Just over 3 percent of active-duty military personnel (67,000) are single parents; about 60 percent are men. Two-fifths of these single parents were deployed to the Persian Gulf, including 4,000 women. The Pentagon has estimated that 6 of the 375 deaths associated with Desert Shield and

---

127. *People*, September 10, 1990, pp. 42–49. See also, "When Dad and Mom Go to War," *Time*, February 18, 1991, p. 69; "When Breadwinners Go Off to Fight," *U.S. News and World Report*, February 25, 1991, p. 69; and Sally Quinn, "Mothers at War: What Are We Doing to Our Kids?" *Washington Post*, February 10, 1991, p. C-1.

128. "Americans Oppose Moms at War," *Washington Times*, February 21, 1991, p. 9.

129. Rick Maze, "House Renews Dependent Debate," *Air Force Times*, May 27, 1991, p. 8.

130. Rick Maze, "Pentagon Backs away from Exemption for Mothers of Infants," *Navy Times*, April 1, 1991, p. 4; and William Matthews, "Senate Votes Down Wider Combat Exemptions," *Air Force Times*, March 4, 1991, p. 16.

131. Department of Defense, "Utilization of American Military Women," p. 9.

Desert Storm were single parents, including one woman.[132] This experience and the resulting public awareness of single-parent personnel, combined with the Pentagon's revisions of assignment regulations should resolve the issue.

All in all, opinion polls show a growing public acceptance of women in the military and, to a lesser extent, women in combat. But these results should be interpreted cautiously. As the report on the Roper survey done for the Herres commission explains,

> That women should be excluded from combat assignments—be they ground, air, or sea assignments—is felt by a minority of the American public. This view is not surprising in light of the nature of public opinion data that Roper has gathered over the years. In a variety of situations, Americans readily support policies which they perceive as allowing people the greatest degree of choice. So, rather than forcing women into combat, or excluding them from such assignments, Americans favor offering the women the right to volunteer or to choose.[133]

Public views about women in combat, however, are strongly influenced by perceptions of risk, and the Persian Gulf conflict presented an unrealistic picture of the potential horrors of the battlefield. The nightly telecasts of the Vietnam war brought vivid scenes of dead and mutilated victims of search-and-destroy firefights into American living rooms. The images of Operation Desert Storm were mainly of smart weapons finding their marks with unprecedented precision. Except for the coverage of Americans captured by the Iraqis and the damage inflicted by Scud attacks, especially the direct hit on a barracks in Dhahran, the American public was spared vivid images of combat action.

Would Congress have so readily repealed the legal barriers had the Persian Gulf conflict resulted in more carnage and terror? Probably not, according to one media observer, who contended that "the Pentagon is faced with this enthusiasm for women warriors because of [news] coverage it controlled. If the war had lasted longer and the number of women killed in action had been greater . . . the public mood toward repealing the exclusions might be far less tolerant than it appears in Washington."[134]

---

132. Data provided by the Office of the Assistant Secretary of Defense for Force Management and Personnel, February 1992.

133. "Attitudes Regarding Assignment of Women . . . Public Perspective," pp. 24–25.

134. Comments attributed to Rod Gilatt, head of the Broadcast News Department, University of Missouri Journalism School, quoted in Alan McConagna, "TV Channeled Women's Greater Role," *Washington Times*, June 18, 1991, p. 1.

Public opinion may be important in determining women's participation in combat, but placing great stock in the results of surveys taken in peacetime among a generally uninformed pool of respondents would be imprudent. It is particularly important to discount public viewpoints that may be based mainly on the Persian Gulf conflict, which by most reckoning, was a distorted model of warfare.

Women and the Draft

With the revival of the debate over women in combat, the question of whether women should be subject to conscription was not far behind. Most surveys indicating public approval of women in combat roles assumed they would volunteer for such duty. But if men can be assigned involuntarily to combat duties, shouldn't women be treated equally? "The issue is not simply 'opening up' combat assignments for military women," according to an eminent sociologist, "the core question is should women soldiers confront the same combat liabilities as men?" Drafting women into combat units, he contends, "could tear the country apart."[135] Although proponents of women in combat consider this argument a red herring and dismiss it as hypothetical, it remains a valid concern. At the very least, flattening the barriers for ground combat duty would raise anew the question of draft registration for women.

Female registration was debated and litigated in 1979–80. Draft registration had been terminated by President Gerald Ford in 1975, but support was once again building in Congress in the late 1970s as the educational attainment and abilities of volunteers plummeted. Many legislators believed the volunteer experiment was about to fail. Initially the Carter administration opposed reinstatement and probably killed any congressional initiatives by suggesting that if registration were revived, women should be included. But in a move that surprised even his own appointed officials, President Carter announced during his State of the Union address on January 23, 1980, his decision to reinstate registration, followed by an announcement on February 8 that he would request authority to include women.[136] The change of heart apparently was prompted by the president's desire to send a signal of resolve to the

135. Charles Moskos, "Women in Combat: The Same Risks as Men?" *Washington Post*, February 4, 1990, p. C7.

136. For a detailed description of these events, see Holm, *Women in the Military*, chap. 23.

Soviet Union, which had just invaded Afghanistan. Including women in the legislative proposal, however, turned many supporters of registration against it, including Senators John Stennis of Mississippi and Sam Nunn of Georgia (who ironically had introduced the legislation on behalf of the administration).

Following a protracted emotional debate, both houses rejected the proposal to register women but authorized funds to register men. The Senate Armed Services Committee made clear its rationale for excluding women: "The policy precluding the use of women in combat is, in the committee's view, the most important reason for not including women in a registration system." The chairman of the House Armed Services Personnel Subcommittee echoed the sentiment: "If [women] are not going to be used in combat, then registration is just a gesture."[137]

But the matter did not rest there. The revival of registration also resurrected a class-action suit brought in 1971 by draft resisters who contended that excluding women from conscription abridged men's rights to equal protection. The case had been dismissed in a lower court, but it was returned by an appeals court in 1973 for reconsideration of the sex discrimination challenge. When the draft was abolished, however, the issue became moot and the case went untried.

Soon after President Carter's call for resuming registration, a district court ruled in the earlier case, declaring that the Military Selective Service Act unconstitutionally discriminated between men and women and was in violation of the Fifth Amendment.[138] The decision was overturned by the Supreme Court in a six to three ruling that Congress had the constitutional authority to exclude women from conscription. This deference to the legislature was not surprising, given the history of Court decisions that pitted equal protection and national security against one another. The question left hanging, however, is what impact would the removal of combat restrictions have on the court's view of future litigation brought on the same basis?

The Herres commission concluded by a vote of eleven to three that "women should not be required to register for or be subject to conscription."[139] This recommendation was consistent with its recommendation that women not be admitted to the ground combat force, historically the principal consumer of a military draft.

137. Quoted in Holm, *Women in the Military*, pp. 363, 364.
138. *Goldberg v. Rostker* (Civil Action No. 71-1480).
139. *Presidential Commission on Assignment of Women*, pp. 40–41.

The Economics of Women in Combat

Critics of an expanded function for women in the armed forces have long contended that the cost of constructing or modifying housing and lavatory facilities to ensure privacy would be prohibitive. In many cases, however, such judgments had been based on views about privacy that, in many parts of American society, became outdated during the 1960s as the feminist movement and sexual revolution took hold. When the number of women in the armed forces first increased, for example, and the services attempted to cling to traditional mores, Air Force policy prevented the joint use of hallways in sexually integrated barracks. But with time the armed forces, at relatively modest cost, modified barracks to an integrated configuration similar in many respects to college dormitories.

In some cases, such as berthing women on naval vessels, the costs have probably been greater. But the Navy has successfully integrated its support fleet, and the marginal costs associated with extending the concept to combat ships should not be prohibitive. Estimates provided to the Herres commission by the Navy in 1992 ranged from $66,000 to accommodate nineteen women on an MHC 51 (mine countermeasure ship) to $2 million to $4 million to modify an aircraft carrier.[140]

For ground combat units, which spend much of their training time in the field, habitability would not seem to rest on cost considerations. Integrated Army barracks are now commonplace, and although privacy and sanitary facilities in the field pose some problems, few were reported during the Persian Gulf deployment.

It is less easy to dismiss costs that could be involved with redesigning equipment to accommodate women. Until recently, military clothing, protective equipment, and work spaces (such as aircraft and tank compartments) have been designed for people with anthropometric dimensions ranging from the 5th through the 95th percentiles of all men. Anyone whose measurements have fallen in the top and bottom 5 percent of the male population has not been accommodated. In a number of critical dimensions—weight, stature, sitting height, eye height, popliteal height (floor to thigh while seated), functional reach, and foot length—the av-

---

140. *Presidential Commission on Assignment of Women*, pp. 38–39. In the mid-1970s the Navy had estimated that it could outfit all of its carriers to accommodate crews of which one-fifth were women for about $400,000 (in 1974 dollars). *Hearings on H.R. 9832, to Eliminate Discrimination Based on Sex with Respect to the Appointment and Admission of Persons to the Service Academies*, House Armed Services Committee, 93 Cong. 2 sess. (GPO, 1974), pp. 118–19.

Table 2-5. *Body Dimensions Considered in Army Aircraft Design, and Percent of Women below Minimum Design Standard*

Body dimension	Percent of women	Body dimension	Percent of women
Bideltoid breadth	75	Span	60
Buttocks-knee length	25	Thumbtip reach, extended	55
Dactylion reach from wall	60	Vertical grip reach	55
Forearm-forearm breadth	60	Vertical grip reach down	55
Functional leg length	40	Wrist–center of grip length	20
Hand length	45	Wrist-thumbtip length	30
Interpupillary breadth	15	Wrist-wall length	55
Sitting height	50		

Source: Claire C. Gordon and others, *1988 Anthropometric Survey of U.S. Army Personnel: Methods and Summary Statistics*, Natick/TR-89/044 (Natick, Mass.: U.S. Army Natick Research, Development, and Engineering Center, September 1989), pp. 96, 124, 178, 182, 190, 208, 258, 268, 284, 323, 332, 334, 370, 426, 428.

erage woman is significantly smaller than the average man. More important, a large proportion of women measure less than men at the 5th percentile. About 50 percent of Army women weigh less than a man at the 5th percentile (136 pounds), 60 percent are shorter (64.8 inches), 50 percent have a shorter sitting height (33.6 inches), and 60 percent have a shorter popliteal height (15.5 inches).[141]

In recent years the rapidly changing demographic composition of the armed forces and the greater career opportunities for women have prompted changes in the military's specifications for clothing and protective equipment, including helmets and body armor, or flak jackets. These items are now designed to encompass a much wider range—the 5th percentile woman through the 95th percentile man.[142] But because there was no reason, until recently, to consider changes in standards for weapon systems, combat aircraft and tracked vehicles in the current inventory have been designed to the male standards. Consequently, relatively fewer women could be expected to operate these systems safely and efficiently. To illustrate, table 2-5 shows the body dimensions typically considered in the design of Army aircraft cockpit systems, along with the proportion of women who would be expected to be anthropometrically incompatible with those systems.

Anthropometric differences would also affect the operation of ground weapon systems. The safe employment of the Stinger air defense missile,

141. Gordon and others, *1988 Anthropometric Survey*, pp. 244, 258, 270, 320.
142. Military Standard 1472 D, notice 2 (Human Engineering Design Criteria for Military Systems, Equipment and Facilities).

for example, requires that the breech of the weapon be at least 30 inches above the ground to avoid the effects of backblast.[143] To fire the missile at a target at 40 degrees elevation under these conditions, the shoulder height of the operator would have to be at least 53 inches, a specification that is met by 95 percent of men but only 40 percent of women.[144]

It is difficult to generalize about the importance of these standards since some could involve mission safety and effectiveness while others could be associated with comfort. Because adherence to the standards has not been universally enforced, there has been a tendency to minimize the risks involved in small deviations. But although differences may appear insignificant, one researcher has warned that "seemingly minor variations of a few centimeters in essential dimensions . . . may be critical determinants in the efficient and safe usage of vehicles and vehicular subsystems, controls, instrument panels, displays, etc., and in the adequate accommodation of some clothing and protective gear."[145]

The costs for widening the anthropometric range for new systems are unclear but are unlikely to be prohibitive. The armed forces may already be revising design standards for future combat systems to accommodate both men and women, but there are no publicly available estimates of the incremental costs associated with expanding the range. The design standards for the C-17 aircraft accommodate the 5th through 95th percentile aviator (man or woman)—the same standards that govern entry into undergraduate pilot training. The Air Force's design for the advanced F-22 fighter reportedly will accommodate virtually all potential applicants, excluding only those falling outside the 0.5 to 99.5 gender-neutral percentile range.[146]

The costs of retrofitting existing systems are even more unclear. The Army does not anticipate substantial modifications to its current fixed-wing inventory, but it estimates that the cost to study the modifications needed in its helicopter fleet would be $750,000. The Air Force, too, seems uncertain about these costs, indicating that aircraft contractors

143. Robert N. Daws, Jr. and others, *Reverse Engineering of the Stinger Air Defense Missile System: Manpower Personnel and Training in the Weapons System Acquisition Process* (Alexandria, Va.: U.S. Army Institute for the Behavioral and Social Sciences, March 30, 1984).

144. Shoulder (or acromial) height comparisons from Gordon and others, *1988 Anthropometric Survey*, p. 76.

145. Monica M. Glumm, "The Female in Military Equipment Design," technical memorandum 13-76 (U.S. Army Engineering Laboratory, April 1976), p. 2.

146. *Presidential Commission on Assignment of Women*, pp. C-90, C-91.

would need to conduct studies and analyses to determine modifications required, if any, and the cost.[147]

In any case, the extent of integration would be an important consideration because the costs would outweigh the benefits if only small numbers of women were involved. Certainly for existing systems, fitting the woman to the machine would be more efficient than fitting the machine to the woman.

The Presidential Commission's Report

The Presidential Commission on the Assignment of Women in the Armed Forces considered many of these issues during deliberations over whether combat restrictions on women should be revised. In the end, the commission recommended that

—women should be permitted to serve on combatant vessels except for submarines and amphibious ships;

—women should continue to be prohibited from serving on combat aircraft and that the sections of the law repealed by Congress in 1992 to permit such assignments be reenacted;

—women should continue to be excluded from ground combat units and positions and that this exclusion, which has been a matter of policy rather than law, be codified.[148]

These recommendations followed often rancorous debate between those for whom military effectiveness was the overarching criterion and those for whom equal opportunity was the predominant consideration. One of the principal cruxes was where, in the absence of empirical data, the burden of proof should lie. Charles Moskos framed the issue succinctly.

> You raised a question, Mr. Chair. . . . Other things being equal, you say, well, then let equal opportunity triumph. Well, most of the evidence that we've heard here—and there will be some debate about the degree—is that mixed-gender units, particularly as they get closer to the combat area, have lower deployment rates, higher attrition, less physical strength, more sexual activity, higher costs, et cetera, et cetera.

147. *Presidential Commission on Assignment of Women*, pp. C-90, C-95.
148. *Presidential Commission on Assignment of Women*, pp. 24–30.

It would seem to me that the burden of proof would be on the side of
saying equal opportunity is of such significance that we're going to override
some of these costs.[149]

The votes on the aircraft and ship restrictions were close calls. The
commission voted eight to seven to continue the restrictions on women
in combat aircraft, with the decisive vote cast by retired Army General
Maxwell R. Thurman, based largely on his concerns about their becoming prisoners of war.[150] Following an admonition by Chairman Robert
Herres to "think carefully about the ramifications of a report that says:
No change; status quo,"[151] the vote to recommend partial removal of the
combat ship restriction was eight to six (with one abstention), as General
Thurman, discounting the POW possibilities for members of ship's crews,
switched sides. Finally, the ban on women in ground combat was upheld
by a lopsided ten to zero (with two abstentions).[152] The meeting at which
the votes were taken was marked by a walkout of five conservative commissioners, who sought to have their views separately incorporated into
the commission report. The report, with a section containing their alternative views, was submitted to the president on November 15, 1992. He
forwarded it, without comment, to Congress on December 15, thus leaving it to the new Clinton administration and Congress to ponder.

In the final analysis, the commission had trouble being taken seriously
owing to a perception, created mostly by feminists and nourished by the
media, that it was stacked with idealogues committed to the status quo.[153]
In a harsh critique of the committee's work, William P. Lawrence, retired
Navy vice admiral and former superintendent of the U.S. Naval Academy,
concluded,

> The most likely future disposition of the Commission's report will be
> transmission to the National Archives for review by scholars and, unfor-
> tunately, not much else. The new President, Secretary of Defense, and the
> Congress must start over again on addressing the question of women in

149. *Presidential Commission on Assignment of Women*, pp. 47–48.
150. *Presidential Commission on Assignment of Women*, p. 87. "The idea that we would
position women in the arena of being subjected to violence, death, depravity as prisoners
is one I won't sign up to," he said. Barton Gellman, "Panel Seeks to Limit Women in
Combat: Presidential Commission Divided," *Washington Post*, November 4, 1992, p. A3.
151. Grant Willis, "Panel 'Inflames the Debate' on Women," *Navy Times*, November
16, 1992, pp. 4, 27.
152. *Presidential Commission on Assignment of Women*, p. 27.
153. See, for example, John Lancaster, "Combat Panel Feels Heat of Political Combat,"
Washington Post, October 9, 1992, p. A25; and George C. Wilson, "Next Women's Panel
Should Quell Its Showboating," *Air Force Times*, November 30, 1992, p. 31.

combat. It is highly regrettable that not only has $4 million of the taxpayers' money been largely wasted, but our country has missed a golden opportunity to intelligently and comprehensively focus on an important national issue.[154]

In fact, the split between the military effectiveness and equal opportunity factions was fairly even, with the close votes decided by a handful of centrist commissioners. The politics behind the appointments and the bizarre circumstances surrounding the final votes may have diminished the credibility of the commission, but a large body of information was collected that, with appropriate analysis, could contribute meaningfully to the ongoing debate.

Narrowing the Uncertainties

A common thread through much of the analysis in this chapter has been uncertainty. Given the absence of empirical data, the issue of whether to allow women into combat, especially ground combat, eludes theoretical solution and forces a much greater reliance on educated speculation based on tradition, anecdotal information, military judgment, and, in some cases, guesswork. It may seem unfair to base decisions on such a shaky foundation, but most informed observers (including the diverse members of the presidential commission) agree that the barriers to women serving in ground combat positions, at least for the time being, should remain in place.

If, however, as many believe, it is inevitable that the issue will be reconsidered sometime, it would be useful to conduct experimental programs *now* to ensure that better data are available for a more informed debate. The exact specifications of a test program would have to be worked out between Congress and the Pentagon, but certain broad principles should govern the experiment. The test should be limited to ensure that combat effectiveness is not unduly compromised, but it should be sufficiently extensive to provide a valid sample.

The design of such an experiment would have to be carefully considered. Criteria for selection, classification, and assignment of personnel, both men and women, would be important, as would the measures of effectiveness to be used. Particular attention would have to be paid to

154. William P. Lawrence, "The Commission," *Naval Institute Proceedings*, February 1993, p. 51.

the proportions of men and women in the units. The military services would have to redirect current recruiting practices to publicize these openings: one important facet of the test would be to find out how many women would be willing to serve in ground combat units. Military planners would have to develop realistic physical and aptitude standards and methods to measure people's ability to meet them.

Tests involving the integration of women into aviation and armor or mechanized units would be especially difficult to devise because relatively few women would be able to meet the anthropometric standards for operating current helicopters, tanks, and armored personnel carriers. It could well turn out that the number of women who would volunteer for combat duty, who could meet the appropriate physical and aptitude standards, and whose body measurements were compatible with the weapon systems employed in ground combat units would be too small to warrant the tests.

Finally, if tests are to be conducted, the criteria for assessing the comparative effectiveness of integrated and nonintegrated units would have to be established. Because measurements would be taken in a peacetime setting, care would have to be exercised in extrapolating women's ability to withstand under wartime conditions the stresses inherent in each category of combat. Assessments of comparative effectiveness should not be expected to meet tests of scientific rigor, since valid measurements of combat performance are so elusive. Rather, the relative proficiency of the units could be evaluated using criteria similar to those now employed at the Army's National Training Center, for example, to measure the effectiveness of all-male combat units.

A valid test program would probably take several years to complete. It would take time to recruit and train women in the necessary skills. Initially, of course, women would be working at the apprentice and journeyman skill levels and in the lower grades, without the senior role models considered important to combat soldier development. This situation would exist at least until women had attained enough training and experience to qualify as noncommissioned officers leading squads and platoons.

CHAPTER THREE

Peacetime Benefits and Wartime Burdens: The Black Dilemma

ONE OF THE MOST striking changes in the nation's armed forces since the end of conscription has been the increased participation by black Americans. Historically, the military had excluded blacks during periods of peace and expediently accepted them during mobilization for war. Thus black Americans for the most part served in proportions smaller than their proportions in the population in peacetime and at or near their proportions in wartime.

This pattern was interrupted with the adoption of the all-volunteer force in 1973. Record numbers of African Americans began entering military service. From the end of the draft to the end of the 1980s their proportion in the armed forces grew from 12 percent to more than 20 percent. The growth was particularly conspicuous in the Army's enlisted ranks, where the share grew from 18 percent to 32 percent.

This development won the approval of many Americans. The armed forces seemed one of the least racially discriminatory institutions in American society, and military service offered a chance for blacks to achieve upward educational, social, and financial mobility. But other observers were more cautious. They warned that the opportunities needed to be weighed against the traditional perils of military service. And they questioned on grounds of morality and equity the disproportionate burden of defense borne by a part of the population that has not enjoyed a fair share of society's benefits.

The warning voices went unheard as long as the nation was at peace, but when developments in the Persian Gulf in 1990 raised the prospect that African Americans might bear the brunt of casualties in a war with Iraq, the calculation changed. The issue was pushed to the forefront as many black leaders expressed concern and social commentators debated the moral and ethical aspects of an unrepresentative military force. The nation, it appeared, might be coming to grips with the trade-off between the benefits and burdens of military service, but the conflict ended with relatively few casualties before the questions could be seriously considered and Americans turned their attention elsewhere. The dilemma, however, remains and needs to be addressed before America becomes involved in another military conflict.

The crucial questions are whether the nation should seek to avoid the potentially divisive effects of disproportionate black casualties in future military conflicts and, if so, how.

The Revolutionary War to Vietnam

Black Americans have a proud tradition of service in the nation's military forces, much of which was suppressed or ignored until the 1960s when the civil rights movement began to raise public consciousness. In retrospect the achievements were remarkable, given the indignities and humiliation, the discrimination, and the stereotypes of racial inferiority that were pervasive until the middle of the twentieth century.

Blacks' participation in the American armed forces began when the colonies established policies concerning the use of slaves in their militias. Initially, fearing slave revolts, they excluded blacks from military service. Gradually, the restrictions were loosened, and some allowed blacks to serve, but only as fifers, drummers, or laborers, none of which required bearing arms. Eventually military necessity compelled some colonies to overlook these restrictions, and some even promised freedom to blacks who performed well in battle. The prospect of freedom attracted many slaves to serve in the colonial forces, and free blacks sought to lift themselves from low social status by distinguished action.[1] In the early days

1. Jack D. Foner, *Blacks and the Military in American History: A New Perspective* (Praeger, 1974), pp. 4–5. Much of the history in this section is adapted from Martin Binkin and Mark J. Eitelberg with Alvin J. Shexnider and Marvin M. Smith, *Blacks and the Military* (Brookings, 1982), pp. 11–38, 75–80.

of the American Revolution, some 5,000 black militiamen fought at Lexington, Concord, Ticonderoga, and Bunker Hill.[2] In the South, meanwhile, the continuing fear of slave revolts prevailed over the exigencies of war; provisions against the enlistment of blacks were sustained.

Following the Revolutionary War, blacks were barred from both the regular armed forces and the state militias. Although some served (against official policy) during the War of 1812, it was not until the Civil War that they were again allowed to bear arms. Early in the war they were excluded from the Union Army because the Lincoln administration was sensitive to reaction in the border states, and military leaders feared that the presence of black soldiers would lower the morale and effectiveness of their units. But in the summer of 1862, as the supply of white volunteers dwindled, however, several Union generals established unauthorized black regiments.

When the Emancipation Proclamation was issued in 1863, black participation was authorized, and the states began actively to recruit black volunteers, which conveniently helped fill their draft quotas. All told, 180,000 blacks served in the U.S. Colored Troops, accounting for 9 to 10 percent of the Union Army and about a quarter of the Navy.[3] If black volunteers in independent and state units are also counted, an estimated 390,000 served in the Civil War, of which perhaps 10 percent lost their lives—a mortality rate almost 40 percent higher than that suffered by white troops.[4]

Following the Civil War, Congress authorized the formation of six black regiments, later reduced to four, in the regular Army. Led by white officers, these units fought Indians and filled outposts in the West. They participated in the charge up San Juan Hill and formed part of General John Pershing's flying column that pursued Pancho Villa in the punitive expedition of 1916–17.[5] These segregated regiments were the only ones in which blacks were permitted to serve, except in a national emergency. They thus had few vacancies: then as now civilian life held relatively few

2. Foner, *Blacks and the Military*, p. 15.
3. Benjamin Quarles, *The Negro in the Civil War* (Little, Brown, 1953), pp. 199, 230. See also Foner, *Blacks and the Military*, p. 47.
4. Ulysses Lee, "The Draft and the Negro," *Current History*, vol. 55 (July 1968), p. 29. Mortality data are from John Hope Franklin, *From Slavery to Freedom: A History of Negro Americans*, 5th ed. (Knopf, 1980), p. 224. These estimates include deaths from all causes—accidents and sickness as well as combat fatalities.
5. Marvin Fletcher, *The Black Soldier and Officer in the United States Army, 1891–1917* (University of Missouri Press, 1974), p. 154.

opportunities for blacks, but the Army provided a steady job and income, food and shelter, basic education, and some social status. Blacks made up 10 percent of total Army strength, roughly their proportion in the civilian population.[6]

When the nation mobilized for World War I, the military draft ensured that blacks in the military would approximately represent the population—at the time 10.7 percent black. About 200,000 blacks served in France during the war, most of them draftees because few were allowed to enlist. Eighty percent were assigned as laborers in supply, stevedore, engineer, and other noncombat units; few saw combat duty in segregated units. About 10,000 served in the Navy, mostly as messmen, stewards, or coal passers in engine rooms. The Marine Corps accepted no blacks.[7] Involvement in the war, some black leaders believed, would mean a brighter future for blacks in American society. According to W. E. B. Du Bois, "if the black man could fight to defeat the Kaiser . . . he could later present a bill for payment due to a grateful white America."[8]

In the 1920s and 1930s the Army adopted quotas intended to keep the racial composition in the ranks roughly proportionate to the overall population, a goal that was not achieved. On the eve of World War II, in fact, the Army's mobilization plan called for 6 percent blacks in the enlisted force, 4 percentage points less than their proportion in the population.[9] The Navy had accepted even fewer blacks as Philippine nationals were recruited to fill messmen and steward positions. No blacks were permitted in the Army Air Corps.[10]

Meanwhile, some African-American leaders were becoming increasingly concerned about discriminatory racial policies and conditions in the

6. Foner, *Blacks and the Military*, pp. 52–55. This is not meant to imply that the participation by blacks in the armed forces was without controversy. Indeed, the early years of the twentieth century were marked by two events that tore the Army apart at its racial seams. The infamous Brownsville Affray in 1906 and the lesser-known, but more violent Houston Riots in 1917 are discussed and primary references cited in Binkin and Eitelberg, *Blacks and the Military*, pp. 15–17.

7. Richard J. Stillman II, *Integration of the Negro in the U.S. Armed Forces* (Praeger, 1968), p. 16. See also Lee Nichols, *Breakthrough on the Color Front* (Random House, 1954).

8. Quoted in Stephen E. Ambrose, "Blacks in the Army in Two World Wars," in Stephen E. Ambrose and James A. Barber, Jr., eds., *The Military in American Society* (Free Press, 1972), pp. 178–79.

9. Richard M. Dalfiume, *Desegregation of the U.S. Armed Forces: Fighting on Two Fronts, 1939–1953* (University of Missouri Press, 1969), p. 23.

10. Binkin and Eitelberg, *Blacks and the Military*, p. 19.

armed forces. They won a victory of sorts in the military draft legislation of 1940, which stipulated that the selection of volunteers and draftees should not discriminate "on account of race or color." At the same time, however, the services retained substantial leeway in developing their own standards for enlistment, through which they could potentially control black participation.[11]

As the prospects for American involvement in war increased in 1940, the Roosevelt administration announced that the percentage of blacks in the Army was to be the same as the percentage in the population, black units were to be established in both combat and noncombat branches of the Army but were to remain segregated, and blacks were to be allowed to attend officer candidate schools.[12] But the proportionality goal was never reached; despite the well-intentioned pronouncements of the administration, the Army leadership believed that the military should not be a laboratory for social experimentation. Black soldiers, in general, were viewed as manpower problems rather than assets. Early in the war, the Navy and Marine Corps avoided the issue altogether by accepting only white volunteers. In 1942, however, both services relaxed their restrictions, and the Marine Corps enlisted blacks for the first time in its history. Even then, only a few saw duty in those services.

Before the war ended, black combat units had seen extensive action. A segregated Army Air Force fighter unit distinguished itself in Europe, but doubts about the fighting abilities of segregated ground combat units were widespread.[13] During the war, more than 900,000 blacks served in the Army, 167,000 in the Navy, and 17,000 in the Marine Corps.[14] At the peak in 1944, there were more than 700,000 in the Army, constituting 8.7 percent of total Army strength, still shy of the 10 percent goal. At war's end, blacks accounted for less than 3 percent of all men assigned to combat duty in the Army; 78 percent were performing duties in quartermaster, engineer, and transportation units. In contrast, 40 percent of white males were assigned to those duties in the Army.[15]

11. For a complete discussion of racial policy during the World War II era, see Ulysses Lee, *The United States Army in World War II, Special Studies: The Employment of Negro Troops* (Office of the Chief of Military History, U.S. Army, 1966).

12. Dalfiume, *Desegregation*, p. 39.

13. For a discussion of this controversy, see Binkin and Eitelberg, *Blacks and the Military*, pp. 20–25.

14. Army figure from Ambrose, "Blacks in the Army," p. 186; Navy and Marine Corps data from Foner, *Blacks and the Military*, pp. 172–73.

15. H. S. Milton, ed., *The Utilization of Negro Manpower in the Army*, report ORO-

The irony of the black experience during World War II was not lost on black leaders: in the struggle against a nation that claimed to constitute a master race, America had maintained a segregated military establishment. Stimulated by the rhetoric and ideological aims of the war, many blacks found cause to reexamine their "place" in American society and pressured the Truman administration and the armed forces for changes in policy.[16]

The end of the war brought the largest and most rapid demobilization in the nation's history, and while most white soldiers wanted to be discharged as soon as possible, many blacks wanted to remain in the armed forces. The military, in spite of any unfair treatment, still offered much better opportunities than the civilian job market. Because proportionately fewer blacks than whites left, blacks made up a growing share of the armed forces.

In 1948, as a result of the pressures brought by black leaders, President Harry Truman issued executive order 9981 declaring that "there shall be equality of treatment and opportunity for all persons in the armed services without regard to race, color, religion, or national origin." The order established a committee, chaired by Charles H. Fahy, former U.S. solicitor general, to oversee implementation of the new policy.[17] Despite the order, the Army leadership resisted the changes. In 1950 the Army Board to Study the Utilization of Negro Manpower (the Chamberlin board) concluded that widespread integration, however desirable as a social goal, and abolition of the 10 percent ceiling would markedly reduce unit morale and combat efficiency.[18] The Army denied that its policies were driven by racial prejudice. Rather it pointed to two conditions over which it had no control: that most whites chose not to associate with blacks and that blacks, through no fault of their own, did not have the skills or education required for many of the Army's occupational specialties.[19]

R-11 (Chevy Chase, Md: Operations Research Office, Johns Hopkins University, 1955), p. 562; and Ambrose, "Blacks in the Army," p. 186.

16. Dalfiume, *Desegregation*, pp. 105–31.

17. Executive order 9981, *Federal Register*, vol. 13 (July 28, 1948), p. 4313.

18. Milton, ed., *Utilization of Negro Manpower*, pp. 579–81.

19. The Fahy committee, in fact, had urged the Army to substitute an achievement quota for its racial quota. The Army, it pointed out, could adjust its minimum aptitude requirements and its physical and moral standards to regulate the number of black enlistments. See memorandum to the president from David K. Niles, February 7, 1950, and supporting documents in Morris J. MacGregor and Bernard C. Nalty, *Blacks in the United States*

The outbreak of the Korean War found a still-segregated Army. But by the middle of 1951, large numbers of blacks had enlisted and constituted a quarter of its recruits. The influx overwhelmed the black training units in the United States and black support units in Korea, forcing the integration of Army basic training centers and the assignment of black soldiers to fill shortages in white combat units.

The services' policies during the Korean conflict had mixed results for the concept of a racially integrated military but by and large historians view the results as presaging the civil rights movement launched a decade later. By the end of the war in 1953, segregated units had been eliminated in the Air Force and Marine Corps, and more than 90 percent of black soldiers in the Army had been assigned to integrated units.[20] But half the Navy's 23,000 blacks still served in the steward's branch. Political pressure encouraged the service to open more occupational specialty groups to blacks and, in 1954, to discontinue its separate recruitment of stewards.[21] Segregation in the military was formally ended in October 1954 with the Pentagon's announcement that all-Negro units had been abolished.[22]

The remainder of the decade was a relatively tranquil period for race relations in the armed forces, but with racism still pervasive in many parts of the country, black service personnel often faced the hostility of civilians in the communities surrounding military installations, especially in the South, and many had difficulty finding decent living accommodations, restaurants, and schools.

Most of these problems went unattended by the Pentagon until the early 1960s, when the Kennedy administration reactivated the President's Committee on Equal Opportunity in the Armed Forces, chaired by attorney Gerhard A. Gesell. In its initial report, submitted in 1963, the Gesell committee addressed itself not only to the racial discrimination in civilian communities surrounding military installations, but brought attention to the reasons blacks served in less than proportionate numbers in the armed services and the factors accounting for continued segregation (or only token integration) in the reserves.[23] In 1964 the Army had

---

Armed Forces: Basic Documents, vol. 11: *Fahy Committee* (Wilmington, Del.: Scholarly Resources, 1977), pp. 1343–45.

20. Lee, "Draft and the Negro," p. 33.
21. Foner, *Blacks and the Military*, p. 193.
22. "Services Abolish All-Negro Units," *New York Times*, October 31, 1954.
23. President's Committee on Equal Opportunity in the Armed Forces, *Equality of*

860,000 enlisted personnel, a number that was to grow to 1.4 million in the next four years as the nation became increasingly involved in the longest and one of the most difficult wars in its history.[24] Racial discrimination once again became a subject of widespread interest and controversy. In contrast with World War II and the Korean conflict, when blacks were largely restricted from filling combat positions and had to "fight for the right to fight," the Vietnam conflict produced claims that blacks were doing more than their fair share of the fighting. Many black leaders and other civil rights champions were now questioning the system that favored the recruitment of blacks. Official Pentagon statistics showed that blacks were more likely than whites to be drafted, sent to Vietnam, serve in high-risk combat units, and be killed or wounded.[25]

Between 1961 and 1966, for example, when blacks constituted 11 percent of the American population age nineteen to twenty-one, they accounted for one out of every five Army combat deaths (table 3-1). This mortality rate was proportionate to the number of blacks in combat units and provided civil rights leaders with the evidence to claim that the military was unjustly using black youth as "cannon fodder for a war directed by whites."[26] Martin Luther King, Jr., advocated a boycott of the war by blacks, claiming that they were "dying in disproportionate numbers in Vietnam," while the leaders of the Congress of Racial Equality, the National Urban League, and other civil rights groups contended that the "imbalance of black Americans in the war" and the "racist policies" of the selective service system, led to a "disproportionate percentage of the burdens" to be placed on young blacks.[27]

Treatment and Opportunity for Negro Military Personnel Stationed within the United States: Initial Report (1963), pp. 5, 12, 14.

24. Binkin and Eitelberg, *Blacks and the Military*, p. 32.

25. These statistics were widely reported in the press. See, for example, "The Draft: The Unjust vs. the Unwilling," *Newsweek*, April 11, 1966, pp. 30–32, 34; "How Negro Americans Perform in Vietnam," *U.S. News and World Report*, August 15, 1966, pp. 60–63; "Democracy in a Foxhole," *Time*, May 26, 1967, pp. 15–19; "King Talk," *National Review*, April 18, 1967, pp. 395–96; and "Negroes Go To War," *Economist*, April 15, 1967, p. 255.

26. Sol Stern, "When the Black G.I. Comes Home from Vietnam," in Jay David and Elaine Crane, eds., *The Black Soldier: From the American Revolution to Vietnam* (Morrow, 1971), p. 221.

27. Robert D. Tollison, "Racial Balance and the Volunteer Army," in James C. Miller III, ed., *Why the Draft? The Case for a Volunteer Army* (Penguin, 1968), p. 149; Paul T. Murray, "Local Draft Board Composition and Institutional Racism," *Social Problems*, vol. 19 (Summer 1971), pp. 129–37; and Lee, "Draft and the Negro," p. 47.

Table 3-1. *Army Combat Deaths in Vietnam, by Race, 1961-72*

| | Number of deaths | | |
Year or period	Blacks	Total	Blacks as percent of total
1961–64	12	185	6.5
1965	186	898	20.7
1966	639	3,073	20.8
1967	730	5,443	13.4
1968	1,220	9,333	13.1
1969	772	6,710	11.5
1970	318	3,508	9.1
1971	110	1,269	8.7
1972	13	172	7.6
1961–66	837	4,156	20.1
1967–72	3,163	26,435	12.0
1961–72	4,000	30,591	13.1

Source: Martin Binkin and Mark J. Eitelberg, with Alvin J. Schexnider and Martin M. Smith, *Blacks and the Military* (Brookings, 1982), p. 76.

Meanwhile, protest movements grew increasingly critical of selective service machinery, prompting the establishment of the National Advisory Commission on Selective Service, which gave "careful study to the effect of the draft on and its fairness to the Negro."[28] In its report, released in February 1967, the commission contended that the various racial, social, and economic groups should bear the risk (or incidence) of death in war and the responsibilities of service in peacetime in rough proportion to their percentage in society.

Reacting to the disproportionately high death rates among blacks in 1965–66, the Pentagon ordered a "cutback in frontline participation by Negroes."[29] According to one Army general, "we deliberately spread out Negroes in component units at a ratio pretty much according to the division total. We don't want to risk having a platoon or company that has more Negroes than whites overrun or wiped out."[30] Casualty statistics were soon affected; the proportion of combat fatalities among blacks dropped in the following year and continued to decrease for the remain-

28. *In Pursuit of Equity: Who Serves When Not All Serve?* Report of the National Advisory Commission on Selective Service (1967), pp. 9–10.

29. Thomas A. Johnson, "The U.S. Negro in Vietnam," *New York Times*, April 29, 1968.

30. "How Negro Americans Perform in Vietnam," *U.S. News and World Report*, August 15, 1966, p. 62.

der of the war (see table 3-1). As it turned out, blacks suffered 13 percent of Army combat deaths during the entire wartime period (1961–72), slightly more than their percentage in the civilian population of the same age and almost the same as that of blacks in the Army's enlisted ranks.

Nonetheless, perceptions of racial discrimination and occasional charges of racial genocide contributed to the racial divisiveness already plaguing the nation in the late 1960s. The collision of social forces—the civil rights movement, the antiwar movement, and the War on Poverty—aroused public emotions and exacerbated racial tensions. In the military, racial incidents became commonplace. Among the most widely publicized were a race riot among prisoners in a stockade in Vietnam in 1968, serious racial clashes at several Marine Corps installations in 1969, incidents aboard naval vessels in the early 1970s, and a four-day riot at Travis Air Force Base, California, in May 1971.[31]

Blacks and the All-Volunteer Force

In 1968 presidential candidate Richard M. Nixon proposed to replace military conscription with an all-volunteer system. Although the proposal was met with wide public acceptance, some critics argued that a volunteer Army would be disproportionately black. They considered the proposal a scheme to use black youth to defend white America, a notion that Nixon, in a radio address given two weeks before the 1968 election, dismissed as "sheer fantasy."[32] This position was reinforced by the Gates commission in its report to the president in 1970. Reacting to concerns that "a disproportionate number of blacks will be in military service," the commission confidently predicted, "the composition of the armed forces will not be fundamentally changed by ending conscription." The commission's best projections were that blacks would constitute about 15 percent of enlisted men in all services combined and 19 percent in the Army. The commission left little room for doubt: "to be sure, these are

31. For a description of these events, see "Riot at Longbinh Stockade Attributed to Racial Acts," *New York Times*, September 4, 1968, p. 38; Robert W. Mullen, *Blacks in America's Wars: The Shift in Attitudes from the Revolutionary War to Vietnam* (Monad Press, 1973), pp. 83–84; Alan L. Gropman, *The Air Force Integrates, 1945–1964* (Office of Air Force History, 1978); pp. 215–16; and Adam Yarmolinsky, *The Military Establishment: Impacts on American Society* (Harper and Row, 1971), p. 344.

32. Richard M. Nixon, "The All-Volunteer Armed Force," radio address, October 17, 1968, quoted in Gerald Leinwand, ed., *The Draft* (Pocket Books, 1979), p. 106.

Figure 3-1. *Blacks as a Percent of Army Accessions and Total Enlisted Personnel, Fiscal Years 1971–92*

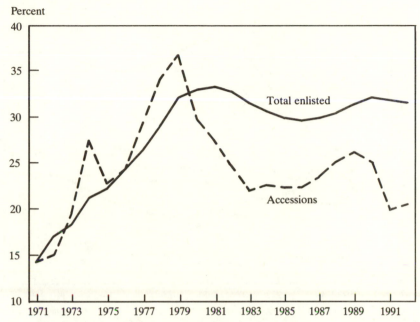

Percent

Total enlisted

Accessions

Sources: Defense Manpower Data Center; and Martin Binkin and Mark J. Eitelberg, with Alvin J. Schexnider and Marvin M. Smith, *Blacks and the Military* (Brookings, 1982), pp. 42, 45.

estimates, but even extreme assumptions would not change the figures drastically."[33]

It soon became evident, however, that the proportion of blacks in the armed forces would grow beyond these predictions. From 1970 to 1973, during the phaseout of compulsory service, the proportion of blacks in the armed forces increased steadily, though modestly, from 9.8 percent to 12.4 percent; in the Army, the proportion increased from 12.1 percent to 16.3 percent. By the mid-1970s it was apparent that the volunteer force was much more attractive to blacks than to whites. The proportion of new Army recruits who were black, for example, grew from 14 percent in 1971 to 24 percent in 1976 (figure 3-1). The trend continued for the remainder of the decade; by 1979 blacks constituted 37 percent of all Army recruits and 32 percent of the total Army enlisted force. The growth in the other services was less dramatic (figure 3-2). Despite a

33. *Report of the President's Commission on an All-Volunteer Armed Force* (GPO, February 1970), pp. 15–16, 149.

Figure 3-2. *Blacks as Percent of Enlisted Personnel, by Service,
Fiscal Years 1971–92*

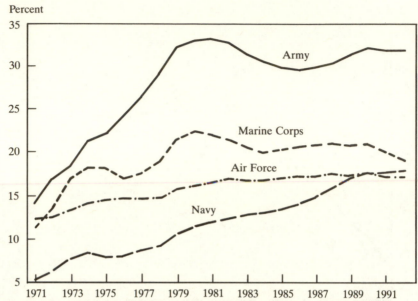

Sources: Data from Defense Manpower Data Center. See also Binkin and Eitelberg, *Blacks and the Military*, p. 42.

doubling of the proportion of black officers, to 5 percent of the total by 1980, the small numbers remained a subject of concern.

The influx of blacks during the 1970s can be attributed to a combination of factors. Most obvious were differences in the civilian employment prospects of white and black youth. The recession of the mid-1970s exacted a relatively greater toll on young black men: their rate of unemployment, already unacceptably high, grew 32 percent between 1973 and 1978, compared with 10 percent growth among white male cohorts (table 3-2). Deteriorating employment prospects are suggested even more vividly by the employment-population ratio, the number of workers as a percentage of the population. Between 1973 and 1978 the ratio for black men dropped by 13 percent; the ratio among white men increased slightly.

The extent to which the military had become a major employer for black youth was evident in their participation rates. During the 1970s nearly 700,000 black men entered the armed forces, 25 percent of all black men who turned eighteen years old. About 230,000, or one-third

Table 3-2. *Unemployment Rates and Employment-to-Population Ratios among 19-Year-Old Men, by Race, Selected Fiscal Years, 1973–90*

Race	1973	1978	1981	1985	1990
Unemployment rate					
White	12.3	13.5	17.9	16.5	14.2
Black	27.8	36.7	40.7	41.0	32.1
Employment-to-population ratio					
White	54.3	56.3	51.3	49.9	51.0
Black	32.8	28.5	24.6	26.3	27.6

Source: *Economic Report of the President, February 1991*, tables B-38, B-40.

of the enlistees, had not completed high school.[34] The contrast appears even starker when one considers that blacks were less likely to qualify for enlistment. By conservative estimate two of every five black men in those age cohorts capable of meeting entry test standards had enlisted, compared with fewer than one of seven similarly situated white men.[35]

By the end of the 1970s, each of the military services had record-high proportions of blacks, with the Army and Marine Corps exceeding the percentage in the American population, the Air Force roughly in proportion, and the Navy slightly underrepresented. This trend, however, failed to concern the American public, according to a survey taken in the early 1980s. In fact, 70 percent of the respondents believed the mix was about right, while 12 percent said there were too many and 19 percent too few.[36] That depressed minorities, especially high school dropouts, were enlisting in disproportionate numbers was apparently viewed as a healthy sign that they could and would receive help. As Milton Friedman, the noted economist, had earlier observed, "it is a good thing and not a bad thing to offer better alternatives to the currently disadvantaged."[37]

In general, the black community appeared ambivalent about the situation. Some leaders were pleased that so many black youth were able

34. A similar proportion of white men who entered the armed forces during the decade had also not completed high school. Data are from Defense Manpower Data Center; and Bureau of the Census, "Preliminary Estimates of the Population of the United States, by Age, Sex, and Race: 1970 to 1981," *Current Population Reports*, series P-25, no. 917 (Department of Commerce, 1982), table 1.

35. The derivation of these estimates is provided in Binkin and Eitelberg, *Blacks and the Military*, p. 66.

36. James A. Davis, Jennifer Lauby, and Paul B. Sheatsley, *Americans View the Military: Public Opinion in 1982*, NORC report 131 (Chicago: National Opinion Research Center, University of Chicago, April 1983), p. 43.

37. Milton Friedman, "The Case for Abolishing the Draft—and Substituting for It an All-Volunteer Army," *New York Times Magazine*, May 14, 1967, p. 118.

to find employment.[38] But not everyone considered the trend so beneficial. Some black leaders complained of continued racial discrimination
in the armed forces, as evidenced by the disproportionate share of disciplinary incidents and punitive actions suffered by racial minorities.[39]
Others criticized imbalance, pointing out that blacks were mired in un-
skilled jobs in the lower ranks. Some decried the relatively small number
of blacks in the officer corps, especially in light of the large numbers in
the enlisted ranks.[40] Although there was some truth to each of the alle-
gations, the armed forces could legitimately point to progress, especially
compared to the dismal conditions outside the military. The comparison
seemed to blunt the sting of the criticisms. On balance, the vestiges of
racial discrimination that had haunted the armed forces in the aftermath
of Vietnam seemed to have disappeared by the end of the 1970s. Those
holding otherwise found themselves a distinct minority.

Meanwhile, some observers attempted to alert the public that while
the military could provide a jobs program and be an engine for social
reform in peacetime, its overarching purpose is to defend the nation.
With memories of Vietnam still fresh, they expressed fears that a racially
unbalanced military could endure black casualties that might exceed
those of the early days of the Vietnam War. If that happened, racial
discord could increase, with potentially damaging consequences for U.S.
national security.[41]

38. One of the strongest proponents for black participation has been Congressman Ronald V. Dellums of California, who chairs the House Armed Services Committee and is a
member of the Congressional Black Caucus. See his article, "Dellums: Don't Slam Door
to Military," *Focus*, vol. 3 (June 1975), p. 6.

39. In 1978 the Southern Christian Leadership Conference blamed black overrepresentation in Army penal facilities on inequities in the criminal justice system, specifically the
low percentage of black officers and the predominance of prejudiced white officers from
the South. Bill Drummond, "Army Concerned about Blacks' High Rates of Criminality,"
Washington Post, November 19, 1978, pp. G1, G2.

40. By 1979, for example, blacks made up 32.2 percent of Army enlisted personnel but
only 6.8 percent of the Army officer corps (Binkin and Eitelberg, *Blacks and the Military*,
p. 42). Much of the disparity resulted from a requirement that officers, with few exceptions,
possess college degrees. In 1979 only 5 percent of all male college graduates age twenty to
twenty-nine were black. Bureau of the Census, "Educational Attainment in the United
States: March 1979 and 1978," *Current Population Reports*, series P-20, no. 356 (Department of Commerce, 1980), table 1.

41. Among the earliest to highlight the issue were Morris Janowitz and Charles C.
Moskos, Jr., "Racial Composition in the All-Volunteer Force," *Armed Forces and Society*,
vol. 1 (November 1974), pp. 109–23; and Binkin and Eitelberg, *Blacks and the Military*
(Brookings, 1982), which drew heavily on Mark Jan Eitelberg, "Military Representation:
The Theoretical and Practical Implications of Population Representation in the American

These two viewpoints illustrate competing perspectives of a thorny issue. On one hand the *benefits* associated with military service should be available to all people regardless of race, color, creed, national origin, or socioeconomic status. On the other hand military service is a *burden* that should be borne by all members of society.

But in the 1980s, perceptions of benefits prevailed; concerns about the possible disproportionate burdens that would be borne by blacks in wartime were confined to a few scholars and social commentators. There was remarkably little public discussion of the racial composition of the armed forces.

The principal exception was a 1982 study that attempted to stimulate interest in the benefits-burden dilemma and promote an informed debate.[42] Some initial reactions to the study were critical or skeptical. In a review for the *Washington Post*, for example, Clifford L. Alexander, Jr., secretary of the Army during the peak years of growth in black participation (1977–81), dismissed the study as "romantic condescension."[43] Nicholas Von Hoffman argued that "history teaches us mercenary soldiers are generally highly reliable" and concluded that "wars should be fought by people who need the work."[44] Carl Rowan, a leading black social commentator, dismissed the prospect that disproportionate black casualties would be socially divisive.

> [The authors] must be joking. Blacks were the "grunts" in the Vietnam War, and they and other minorities and poor whites were the cannon fodder in every other conflict for the simple reason that they always have been powerless to alter this society one whit. . . . They are helpless going into the military, and if they die in combat their relatives will be impotent when it comes to raising a ruckus big enough to be called "socially divisive."[45]

Despite the early criticism and skepticism, a comprehensive discussion of the questions took place at a symposium conducted in 1982 by the Joint Center for Political Studies, a research organization focusing on black issues. Scholars, current and former public officials, and represen-

---

Armed Forces," Ph.D. dissertation, New York University, 1979. Eitelberg's work is the most comprehensive and insightful examination of issues involving representation in the armed forces.

42. Binkin and Eitelberg, *Blacks and the Military*.

43. Clifford L. Alexander, Jr., "In the Army Now," *Washington Post Book World*, August 22, 1982, p. 3.

44. Nicholas Von Hoffman, "Black GIs: A Khaki Quota?" *Philadelphia Daily News*, July 30, 1982.

45. Carl Rowan, "No One's Worried about 'Grunts,'" *Atlanta Constitution*, July 2, 1982.

tatives of major civil rights organizations discussed the issues related to the growing participation of blacks in the armed forces. Although no attempt was made to reach a consensus, the group seemed resigned that little could be done or should be done to alter course. The general tenor of the meeting was summed up by Roger Wilkins: "In the end, the problem of equity and all the other problems that seem to worry people so—readiness, reliability, the reactions of the allies—must await a time when the focus shifts away from the military and toward the society that produced it and that it is supposed to protect."[46]

On the whole, the nation's black leadership remained silent, as did the coalition of liberal and conservative commentators that had expressed concern in the 1970s with the growing participation of blacks in the armed forces. Racial representation in the armed forces, had become a non-issue. "What, if anything, the Pentagon, Congress or the White House should do about the high percentage of minorities in the military," one observer commented in 1983, "might be an important subject for debate—if there were a debate."[47]

Perhaps the public's apathy stemmed from a belief that, despite the Iranian hostage crisis and the Soviet occupation of Afghanistan, the United States would not soon get involved in a major conflict producing high casualties. By most perceptions in the early 1980s, the benefits of military service far outweighed the burdens.

The proportion of blacks in the military appeared to become even less relevant during the Reagan presidency as the armed forces found recruiting far easier, which resulted in fewer new black recruits and the prospect that a more racially balanced force was in the offing. Large increases in pay in 1980 and 1981, totaling 29 percent, improved the attractiveness of military service, especially since civilian wages in many comparable occupations were dropping in real terms.[48] The reintroduction of more

46. Roger Wilkins, "Right Issues, Wrong Questions," in Edwin Dorn, ed., *Who Defends America? Race, Sex, and Class in the Armed Forces* (Washington: Joint Center for Political Studies Press, 1989), p. 164. This book compiled the papers and remarks presented at the 1982 symposium. Wilkins' comment about the reaction of allies was aimed at the revelation by Lawrence J. Korb, then an assistant secretary of defense, that officials of some allied nations, most notably the Federal Republic of Germany, had expressed concerns over the growing number of black American servicemen in their countries. Lawrence J. Korb, "The Pentagon's Perspective," in Dorn, ed., *Who Defends America?* p. 23.

47. Michael R. Gordon, "Black and White," *National Journal*, June 4, 1983, p. 1182.

48. Office of the Secretary of Defense, *Military Compensation Background Papers, Compensation Elements and Related Manpower Cost Items: Their Purposes and Legislative Backgrounds*, 4th ed. (Department of Defense, November 1991), p. 43.

liberal education benefits, similar to those in the Vietnam-era GI bill, also drew more recruits—the especially generous Army College Fund gave the Army a competitive edge. The services also appeared to have adopted better recruiting practices, deploying recruiters more efficiently and employing more imaginative advertising and recruiting techniques. Finally, the image of the armed forces improved, a development attributed by some to the pro-military attitude of the Reagan administration.

The net result was an increase in interest in military service among white youth, a growth in their participation rate, and an attendant decline in the number and the proportion of new black recruits (see figure 3-1). Compared with the 700,000 black men that had entered the armed forces during the 1970s, some 460,000, or 17 percent of those turning eighteen, entered during the 1980s.[49] In fiscal year 1990, blacks constituted 25 percent of Army recruits, down from a peak 37 percent in 1979.

The opportunities were especially diminished for high school dropouts because the services were able to attract record numbers of high school graduates. In the 1970s, for example, 230,000 black male dropouts entered the military services; only 25,000 were accepted during the 1980s. In fiscal year 1990, of a total of the 45,000 blacks who entered the armed forces, only 1,200 (less than 3 percent) had not completed high school.

Despite this substantial decrease, however, the overall racial composition of the Army was hardly affected, hovering near 30 percent black during the decade (see figure 3-2). The seeming anomaly is explained by the fact that even though whites entered the Army in growing numbers during the 1980s, they were less likely to remain beyond an initial enlistment. Blacks have traditionally exhibited a greater desire to remain in the military and have accounted for a larger proportion of reenlistments (figure 3-3).

One consequence of these trends has been that black soldiers are now more concentrated in the middle and upper ranks. Their proportion in the lowest three grades (E-1 through E-3) dropped from almost 32 percent in 1981 to 24 percent in 1991, while the proportion in the highest three grades (E-7 through E-9) grew from less than 25 percent to more than 30 percent (figure 3-4). Blacks in the middle three grades in these years remained at roughly 36 percent of the total.

---

49. Derived from data provided by the Defense Manpower Data Center; and Bureau of the Census, "Projections of the Population of the United States: 1977 to 2050," *Current Population Reports*, series P-25, no. 704 (Department of Commerce, 1977), table 8.

Figure 3-3. *Blacks as Percent of Army Enlistments and Reenlistments, Fiscal Years 1971–90*

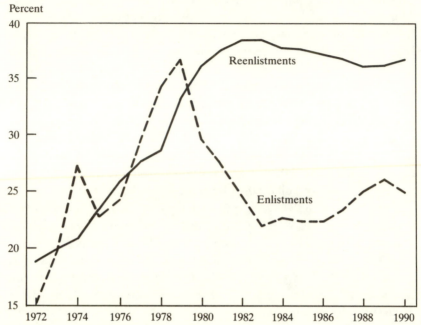

Percent

Sources: Data from Defense Manpower Data Center. See also Binkin and Eitelberg, *Blacks and the Military*, table B-2; and figure 3-1.

The dramatic growth in the participation by blacks since the end of the military draft has been accompanied by modest improvements in their occupational opportunities. In the early 1970s, black soldiers were greatly underrepresented in technical positions and slightly overrepresented in combat billets. They now fill a nearly proportional share of technical jobs and are slightly underrepresented in combat skills (figure 3-5). The most conspicuous change has occurred in health and administration; blacks now hold 45 percent of those jobs in the Army.

Whatever concerns might have existed about the potential burdens of military service all but evaporated in the late 1980s with the crumbling of communism and the disintegration of the Warsaw Pact, events that made even more remote the possibility of American involvement in a large-scale conflict. In fact, Pentagon plans to cut the size of the armed forces by 25 percent were met with questions about the racial implications of such a steep reduction. The nation's black leadership was once again

Figure 3-4. *Distribution of Blacks in Army's Enlisted Ranks, Fiscal Years 1971, 1981, 1991*

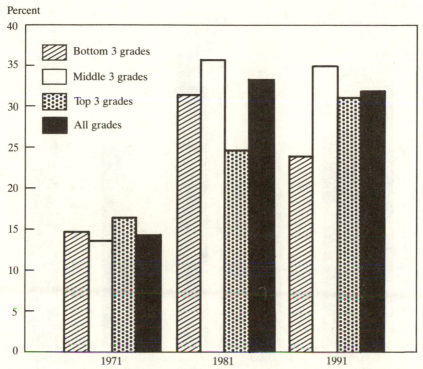

Percent

Legend:
- Bottom 3 grades
- Middle 3 grades
- Top 3 grades
- All grades

Source: Data from Defense Manpower Data Center.

ambivalent. Several leading commentators worried that blacks would bear the economic brunt of the impending reductions, while the Congressional Black Caucus, made up of twenty-four black members of Congress, urged the Pentagon to hasten the pace of the reductions, arguing that "military service should not be looked on as a jobs program."[50] Besides, they contended, their plan set aside "conversion" money to assist those separated from the armed forces. The Pentagon's reduction plan, however, was soon shelved by events in the Persian Gulf, which also served to refocus attention from the benefits of military service to its burdens.

50. For a discussion of the caucus's position, see Rowan Scarborough, "Caucus's Plan Could Hit Blacks Hardest," *Washington Times*, April 19, 1990, pp. A1, A8. Also see Edwin Dorn, "Assessing the Peace Dividend," *Focus*, vol. 18 (April 1990), pp. 3–4.

Figure 3-5. *Distribution of Black Army Enlisted Personnel, by Major Occupational Category, Fiscal Years 1972, 1980, 1990*

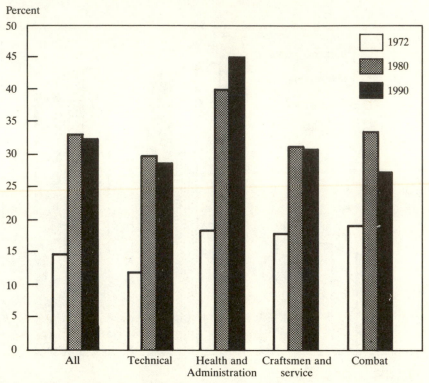

Source: Data from Defense Manpower Data Center.

The Persian Gulf Conflict

President George Bush's commitment in August 1990 to use military power if necessary to eject Saddam Hussein from Kuwait unleashed an almost immediate response from critics, both white and black, worried that the nation's socially unbalanced armed forces would soon be involved in a bloody and distant conflict. The prospect that large numbers of black youths might die commanded wide attention. Although representation of blacks in the armed forces had been growing since the end of the draft, the news media treated the trend as a recent phenomenon that had somehow sneaked up on an unsuspecting public.

Initially, charges of inequity were leveled in terms of social class. The armed forces, some scholars and journalists contended, consisted mainly of the lower socioeconomic classes in American society. These views were based in large measure on an assessment by Charles Moskos, the nation's preeminent military sociologist, who contended in 1988 that "whatever one's value judgment on the [all-volunteer force], the irreducible fact remains that without a citizen-soldier component, the most privileged elements of our youth population . . . will not be found in the enlisted ranks of the armed forces."[51] A report by the Democratic Leadership Council concluded that "we cannot ask the poor and underprivileged alone to defend us while our more fortunate sons and daughters take a free ride, forging ahead with their education and careers."[52] Ethical considerations aside, some argued that if the children of government officials, legislators, corporate leaders, journalists, and other prominent people were put at risk, policymakers' decisions to commit U.S. military forces might be taken more soberly. Moskos, for example, lamented that there were no "future George Bushes in the ranks in the gulf. . . . These are working-class youth, not the future leaders of the country. And they don't have much of a voice in the making of policy."[53]

These claims were dismissed in a 1991 Pentagon report as assertions "based on impressions and anecdotes rather than on systematic data." Synthesizing four independent studies of the socioeconomic composition of the armed forces, the report concluded that "the socioeconomic background of new recruits nearly mirrors that of youth in society."[54] These differences of opinion stemmed from critics' failure to account for the significant changes that had taken place in the services during the 1980s and from the absence of an accepted definition of social classes. What, after all, is the middle class? The Pentagon's report used educational

51. Quoted in Democratic Leadership Council, *Citizenship and National Service: A Blueprint for Civic Enterprise* (Washington, May 1988), p. 25.

52. Democratic Leadership Council, *Citizenship and National Service*, p. 25. Ironically, Governor Bill Clinton, who would become embroiled in the draft controversy during his presidential campaign, was a member of the governing board of the Democratic Leadership Council and one of the architects of its national service proposal. In effect, the council's report appeared at odds with Governor Clinton's credentials for president by asking, "how can [America's future] leaders be expected to grasp the complexities of defense policy without any first-hand experience with the military?" (p. 25).

53. Quoted in Scott Shepard, "Who Dies? Racial Makeup of Gulf Troops Revives Issue of Fairness," *Atlanta Journal*, December 17, 1990.

54. Office of the Assistant Secretary of Defense for Force Management and Personnel, *Population Representation in the Military Services, Fiscal Year 1990* (Department of Defense, July 1991), pp. 33, 41.

attainment, marital status, employment status, home ownership, and occupation of the parents of the groups surveyed to construct a socioeconomic index score.

A Congressional Budget Office study, based on analysis of recruit's ZIP codes came to a similar conclusion: "the socioeconomic characteristics of recruits' home areas are broadly similar to those of the general youth population, although recruits tend to come from areas with somewhat lower family incomes and education levels."[55] As more and more information surfaced debunking the notion that the military was filled with the poor and disadvantaged, social commentators turned their attention toward the racial imbalance in the armed forces—criticism more difficult to dismiss.

American involvement in the Persian Gulf was almost immediately cast in racial terms by a number of prominent black leaders. As had been predicted a decade earlier, the prospect of a great many black casualties was high on the list of concerns.[56] The likelihood, too, that a Persian Gulf conflict would be financed at the expense of social programs loomed large. And the apparent readiness of the United States to engage Arabs, or "people of color," to protect oil interests, while winking at similarly egregious acts by the white South African government, did not sit well with many blacks. The final straw, it appeared, was President Bush's decision to engage in a military ground action that could put many young blacks in harm's way while at the same time vetoing the Civil Rights Bill of 1990.

Among the most vocal black critics of the decision, Jesse L. Jackson warned, "if that war breaks out, our youth will burn first," and Coretta Scott King, branding the United States as the aggressor, "strongly deplore[d] and was deeply saddened by the White House decision to launch a war against Iraq." Eleanor Holmes Norton, delegate to Congress from the District of Columbia, condemned the war and dismissed the contention that black youth might have joined the armed forces for any but economic reasons.[57] Martin Luther King III urged blacks not to partici-

55. Richard L. Fernandez, *Social Representation in the U.S. Military* (Congressional Budget Office, October 1989), p. xii. Also see Fernandez, "A Poor-Man's Military? Not At All," *Washington Post*, December 18, 1990, p. 21.

56. Edwin Dorn, "Devil's Bargain in the Front Lines," *Los Angeles Times*, December 4, 1990, p. B7. Also see Lynne Duke, "For Many Blacks, Call to Duty Rings of Inequality," *Washington Post*, November 28, 1990, p. 1; and Shepard, "Who Dies?"

57. Juan Williams, "Race and War in the Persian Gulf . . . Why Are Black Leaders Trying to Divide Blacks from the American Mainstream?" *Washington Post*, January 20,

pate: "Every black soldier ought to say: 'You all do what you want to. I'm not going to fight. This is not my war.'"[58]

That black service personnel were mostly high school graduates from middle- or working-class families—the "flower of black youth"—was also a source of concern. Representatives of the African American community commented that great numbers of young black men had already been lost to drugs and crime; the community could not afford to lose more in a war. A leader of the National African-Americans against United States' Intervention in the Gulf, for example, protested that "the stabilizing forces in our community are being drawn out."[59]

This divisive rhetoric, coming as it did from some of the most influential black leaders, could have been responsible for shaping the antiwar attitudes of much of black America. A *Wall Street Journal*/NBC News poll conducted shortly after President Bush decided to send military forces to the Persian Gulf showed that 74 percent of white Americans approved the action but only 41 percent of black Americans did so.[60] In January 1991 as war loomed closer, black support dropped to 27 percent before rising to about 50 percent after the war began.[61]

President Bush's deliberations over whether to use military force or economic sanctions to drive Iraqi troops out of Kuwait took place amid widespread news coverage reflecting deep concerns among white and black Americans over the possibilities of heavy casualties. This prospect had to weigh heavily in the president's calculations, but there is no evidence that he recognized, much less was influenced by, the racial component of the issue.

The administration, it is worth noting, enjoyed a distinct advantage in having as its top military leader the first black ever to have held that position. As point man for the administration, General Colin Powell insulated it from some of the criticisms of the black community. Responding to concerns about the potential for disproportionate black casualties, Powell expressed his annoyance: "What you keep wanting me to say is that this is disproportionate or wrong. I don't think it's disproportionate

---

1991, p. B2. Williams, a syndicated columnist, criticized these leaders for driving a "wedge between black America and its troops in combat as well as mainstream America."

58. Isabel Wilkerson, "Blacks Wary of Their Big Role in Military," *New York Times*, January 25, 1991, p. 1.

59. Wilkerson, "Blacks Wary," p. 1.

60. James M. Perry, "Black Voters Are More Disapproving Than Whites of the Deployment of U.S. Forces to Middle East," *Wall Street Journal*, August 22, 1990, p. A10.

61. Williams, "Race and War in the Persian Gulf," p. B2.

or wrong. I think it's a choice the American people made when they said have a volunteer Army and allow those who want to serve to serve." Expressing pride that blacks volunteer for the armed forces in disproportionate numbers, Powell contended that they are drawn to military service for the same reasons that he was as a youth. "They come in for education. They come in for adventure. They come in to better themselves."[62]

Deployments and Casualties

As deployments commenced, many journalists closely monitored racial proportions, prompting the Pentagon to release a fact sheet in January 1991 showing that the racial and ethnic composition of deployed personnel, although overrepresentative of civilian racial and ethnic populations was remarkably close to their participation in the military services (figure 3-6).[63]

Of some 570,000 military personnel deployed between August 1990 and February 1991, 23.5 percent were black, compared with 20.5 percent of the total military population.[64] Most deployed personnel were Army troops, who closely mirrored the overall Army population. The Pentagon also indicated that 36 percent of deployed black personnel were in a combat status, compared with 42.7 percent of the total deployed forces.

As the possibility of a military confrontation loomed larger, concerns about casualties mounted. Experts offered predictions ranging from several hundred to 45,000.[65] There seemed little reason to believe that blacks would not suffer casualties at least in proportion to their numbers in Army combat specialties (27 percent) and possibly in proportion to their numbers in the theater of operations (23.5 percent). As matters turned out, of the 375 persons who died during the buildup (Desert Shield) and

62. Lynne Duke, "Gen. Powell Notes Military Enlistment Remains Matter of Individual Choice," *Washington Post*, November 28, 1990, p. A30.

63. Department of Defense, "Fact Sheet," Desert Shield 153, January 3, 1991.

64. Mark J. Eitelberg, "A Preliminary Assessment of Population Representation in Operations Desert Shield and Desert Storm," paper prepared for the 1991 Biennial Conference of the Inter-University Seminar on Armed Forces and Society, pp. 15, 17, 18; and Defense Manpower Data Center.

65. Les Aspin, chairman of the House Armed Services Committee, estimated that total casualties would be 3,000 to 5,000 with up to 1,000 deaths; Molly Moore, "Aspin War Would Start with Air Strikes, Escalate to Ground Battles," *Washington Post*, January 9, 1991, p. A15. The Center for Defense Information, assuming a 120–day campaign, predicted 45,000 U.S. casualties, including 10,000 deaths. Juan J. Walte, "One Estimate: 45,000 U.S. Casualties," *USA Today*, January 7, 1991, p. 8.

Figure 3-6. *Racial and Ethnic Distribution of Enlisted Personnel Deployed to the Persian Gulf Area, by Service, August 1990– February 1991*

Percent

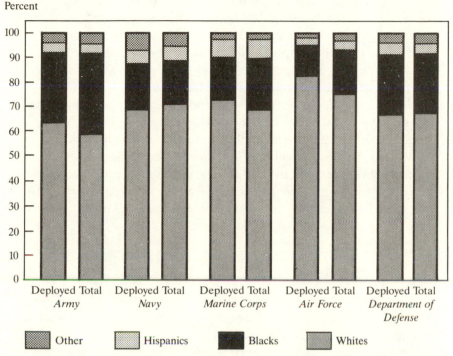

Deployed Total *Army*   Deployed Total *Navy*   Deployed Total *Marine Corps*   Deployed Total *Air Force*   Deployed Total *Department of Defense*

Other   Hispanics   Blacks   Whites

Sources: Mark J. Eitelberg, "A Preliminary Assessment of Population Representation in Operations Desert Shield and Desert Storm," paper prepared for the 1991 Biennial Conference of the Inter-University Seminar on Armed Forces and Society, p. 17; and Defense Manpower Data Center.

the campaign (Desert Storm), 63 (16.8 percent) were black.[66] The proportions were lower than expected because a difficult ground campaign never materialized. The Iraqi army, apparently demoralized by a relentless allied bombing campaign, offered little resistance, and those units that did were readily defeated. Of the 375 American deaths, 148 were the result of combat activity, and 108 were attributed to accidents and illnesses that occurred before hostilities began.[67] Most casualties occurred among troops that were assigned to support rather than combat duties.

66. Eitelberg, "Preliminary Assessment," pp. 17, 32; and data from Defense Manpower Data Center.

67. Nearly a quarter of the combat deaths, according to one report, were the result of friendly fire. Eric Schmitt, "U.S. Seeks to Cut Accidental War Death," *New York Times*, December 9, 1991, p. 12. See also Eitelberg, "Preliminary Assessment," pp. 28, 31.

U.S. casualties would have been much higher and the proportion among blacks larger if the ground war had unfolded as most experts expected. Had the Iraqis resisted as resolutely as had been predicted, casualties among Army and Marine Corps combat troops would have been higher, certainly outnumbering those among support personnel, and most likely increasing the proportion borne by black personnel.[68]

Because the protest against military action by many influential black leaders appeared to resonate throughout much of the black community, heavy black casualties probably would have reinforced their criticisms, further eroding support for the administration's policy and further straining relations between white and black Americans at a time when, by many accounts, the gap between the races has been widening. As matters turned out, the small number of black casualties brought a sudden end to the controversy. With the end of the conflict, in fact, the prewar plan to reduce the size of the armed forces was reactivated and fears that blacks would become wartime casualties were displaced by concerns that they would become economic casualties.[69]

Options for Change

If the clean and decisive Persian Gulf victory is accepted as a model for future military conflicts, there is a great temptation to ignore the seemingly intractable benefits-burdens dilemma. Realistically, however, any future conflict would likely be a tougher test for America's armed forces, probably producing a larger number of casualties and prompting

68. Even in the event of stronger Iraqi resistance, it is unlikely that blacks would have suffered casualties in the same high proportion as their presence in ground combat units because they tend to be clustered in units that have traditionally had less hazardous duties. For example, in 1990 blacks accounted for 23 percent of soldiers assigned to infantry, armor, and combat engineer skills, which in previous wars have accounted for over 93 percent of Army battle losses. But they fill 44 percent of artillery positions, which have accounted, at most, for 7 percent of casualties. See *Planning Factors*, Student text 101-2 (Fort Leavenworth, Kans.: Army Command and General Staff College, June 1985), p. 4-25; and data from Defense Manpower Data Center. Thus if history is a guide, it could be expected that black casualties would have amounted to 22 percent of the casualties taken by ground combat units, a percentage smaller than that of blacks in the combat arms or in the ground forces, but still much larger than in the military-age population as a whole.

69. For example, in August 1991 the *New York Times* was once again reporting that blacks stood to lose the most from the renewed force reductions. Lee A. Daniels, "With Military Set to Thin Ranks, Blacks Fear They'll Be Hurt Most," *New York Times*, August 7, 1991, p. 1. Also see James E. Ellis, "Where Troop Cuts Will Be Cruelest," *Business Week*, June 8, 1992, pp. 72–73.

the reemergence of the debate on racial equity. Any resulting racial discord could hamper the nation's ability to pursue what on all other grounds might be considered a just war. Are these prospects of sufficient concern to warrant considering interventionary policies to redress racial balance in the armed forces? If so, what options are available?

Back to Conscription?

Shortly after the U.S. military buildup on the Arabian peninsula began, some social commentators were calling for a reinstitution of the draft to redress socioeconomic or racial imbalances in the all-volunteer force.[70]

The advocates of a return to the draft, however, were short on details of how conscription would yield a socioeconomically or racially representative military force. They also failed to consider the disposition of the many young Americans who now volunteer for military service. Conscripts would make up the difference between the total need for new recruits and the total number of volunteers. The overall racial characteristics of recruits would depend on the composition of each group and their relative sizes. Also, the demographic profile of the career force is not a mirror image of the profile of new recruits, a fact that seemed to be lost on the advocates.

For a conscription system to affect the racial composition of the total recruit population, either the number of military volunteers must be severely curtailed or the total strength of the armed forces must be greatly

70. Mark Shields, a liberal political and social commentator, lamented that the military buildup on the Arabian peninsula had not touched the Washington establishment. "This noisy, contentious city turned mute because almost without exception no Washington dinner party guest—liberal or conservative, Democrat or Republican—personally knows a single one of the 1.8 million enlisted Americans serving in our armed forces." Mark Shields, "Bellicose Hypocrites," *Washington Post*, November 2, 1990, p. 25. See also John Kenneth Galbraith, "(Class) War in the Gulf," *New York Times*, November 7, 1990, p. A31; and Richard Lacayo, "Why No Blue Blood Will Flow," *Time*, November 26, 1990, p. 34. Finally, the *Boston Globe*, in an editorial opinion, called for a revival of conscription "for reasons of social and economic fairness." "It's Time to Think about the Draft," *Boston Globe*, February 4, 1991, p. 10.

Various groups that opposed the military intervention were quick to join the crusade in hopes the threat of conscription would reignite the "Hell no, we won't go!" rallying cry of the 1960s' campus counterculture that had been widely credited with hastening the end of U.S. involvement in Southeast Asia. See, for example, Michael deCourcy Hinds, "Confrontation in the Gulf: Antiwar Effort Buds Quickly, Nurtured by Activism of 60's," *New York Times*, January 11, 1991, p. A1; and Anthony DePalma, "War in the Gulf: On Campus: A War again Stirs Anguish, But of a Quieter Kind," *New York Times*, January 20, 1991, p. 18A.

increased. To illustrate, in fiscal year 1990 the Army recruited 80,000 volunteers, of which 20,000, or 25 percent, were black. Assuming that the number of volunteers was reduced by one-third and the shortage made up with conscripts, the percentage of black recruits would drop only to 20 percent—still well above their numbers in the overall population.[71] Even then, because the armed forces have successfully met their needs for volunteers for more than a decade, it must be assumed that a reduction in volunteers would have to be *induced* by adopting policies that would either discourage enlistments (perhaps by lowering military pay) or would accept fewer applicants (perhaps by tightening entry standards). Realistically, however, such measures would have to be justified on their own merits; a policy that denied youths an opportunity to serve *voluntarily* in order to force others to serve *involuntarily*, solely for the purpose of achieving racial balance, is not likely to be socially and politically acceptable.

Alternatively, a more representative racial balance could be achieved without denying volunteers the opportunity to serve by increasing the size of the force. The racial composition of the force, however, would not be highly sensitive to changes in strength. If the number of Army recruits were increased by 25 percent (80,000 to 100,000) to make room for 20,000 conscripts, blacks would then be expected to constitute 22 percent rather than 25 percent of Army recruits. Thus for an appreciable change to take place, total recruit requirements would have to be increased to a level at which the racial composition of conscripts would swamp the composition of volunteers. This option, too, is unrealistic in light of plans to contract rather than expand the armed forces.

Attaining racial balance among the recruit population, in any event, does not ensure attaining it in the overall military population. As figure 3-3 showed, once in the armed services, blacks are more likely than whites to remain beyond the first tour of duty. Of all male recruits who entered the Army between April 1981 and March 1982, 18 percent of the

71. Data from Defense Manpower Data Center. This assumes that the smaller group of volunteers would have the same racial distribution and that conscripts would be provided by a stochastic, or lottery, system with few exemptions and deferments, which in theory would provide a representative cross-section of the eligible population. It should be noted that blacks would be underrepresented in a randomly selected draft population because they would be less likely to meet minimum entry standards. For example, blacks make up about 15 percent of 18–year-old men, but under existing entry standards only 11 percent would be *eligible* for military service. See Fernandez, *Social Representation in the U.S. Military*, p. 78.

whites but 31 percent of the blacks were still in the Army as of July 1988.[72] The greater tendency of blacks to reenlist accounts for the fact that, while the proportion of Army recruits who were black was falling from 37 percent in 1979 to 20 percent in 1991, the proportion of blacks in the Army's enlisted ranks changed little, hovering between 30 and 33 percent (see figure 3-1). Little would be different under conscription, moreover, because blacks could be expected to be concentrated in the volunteer component of a mixed volunteer-conscript force, and volunteers typically remain in the service longer than draftees.

It is therefore difficult, under the circumstances, to imagine any realistic conscription plan that would yield a racially representative force. Besides, with the end of the cold war any conceivable rationale for a return to conscription has virtually disappeared, and it is unlikely that a military draft would be reinstated solely to meet a social purpose.

Redressing Racial Balance in the Volunteer Force

Attaining a more representative force under current volunteer conditions rather than conscription would also be no mean task. One eminent black scholar has recommended a direct approach: *"The Congress should establish a goal of proportionate participation in the military for minorities."*[73] But such extreme views are not widely embraced and, whatever euphemism is used, any approach that even hints at quotas is unlikely to gain support from legislators or policymakers. Left to market forces, then, the racial composition in the future, as in the past, will rest on the relative propensities of black and white youth for military service.

Preferences for military service are shaped by many factors, but most prominently by the availability of alternative employment opportunities.[74] It is therefore difficult to envision major changes in preference patterns, at least in the short run, given the existing imbalances in the

72. Fernandez, *Social Representation in the U.S. Military,* pp. 64–65.

73. "Prepared Statement of Dr. Ronald Walters" in *The Impact of the Persian Gulf War and the Decline of the Soviet Union on How the United States Does Its Defense Business,* Hearings before the House Armed Services Committee, 102 Cong. 1 sess. (GPO, 1991), p. 135. Walters, a professor of political science at Howard University, suggested that a limitation be placed on the number of enlistments that could be accepted from certain "economically impacted communities" (p. 135).

74. The close connection between voluntary enlistments and civilian employment opportunities has been verified in countless econometric studies. For example, see Charles Dale and Curtis Gilroy, "The Effects of the Business Cycle on the Size and Composition of the U.S. Army," *Atlantic Economic Journal,* vol. 11 (March 1983), pp. 42–53.

educational attainment, job skills, and employment opportunities. Until these differences are narrowed, military service will continue to be more attractive to blacks than to whites, and there would not appear to be any basis for assuming that the racial composition of the all-volunteer force will change much.

Two developments in the early 1990s, however, suggest that the calculus of racial composition might change: the substantial reductions in the size of the military and signs of a declining propensity for military service among black youths.

DOWNSIZING: IMPLICATIONS AND CHALLENGES. The Pentagon's plan to reduce the size of the armed forces by 25 percent between 1990 and 1995 has taken on racial overtones. Countering concerns expressed among some African American leaders, but mainly by the news media, that blacks would be squeezed out of a smaller military, the Pentagon's leading manpower official told Congress,

> we are convinced that our drawdown plans will not differentially affect minorities or women. We expect they will separate in numbers roughly proportional to their representation in the overall groups that are being separated. Perhaps most to the point, at the end of 1995 when the drawdown is completed, we expect the minority and gender representation figures to be virtually the same as they are today.[75]

The basis for the prediction is, however, unclear, especially in the face of the military services' traditional tendency to upgrade the quality of their work force as their requirement for recruits diminishes.[76] For example, as the Army's needs dropped from 80,000 recruits in 1990 to

75. Testimony by Christopher Jehn, assistant secretary of defense for force management and personnel, in *Hearings on National Defense Authorization Act for Fiscal Years 1992 and 1993—H.R. 2100 and Oversight of Previously Authorized Programs*, Hearings before the Military Personnel and Compensation Subcommittee, House Armed Services Committee, 102 Cong. 1 sess. (GPO, 1991), p. 394.

76. An important measure of the quality of prospective volunteers is the score obtained on the Armed Services Vocational Aptitude Battery (ASVAB). This entry test is used both to measure general military trainability in a single index common to all services and to assess vocational aptitude for job categories specific to each service. Qualification for entry into a service is based on scores obtained on one portion of the battery, called the Armed Forces Qualification Test (AFQT), which place applicants into categories ranging from very high trainability (category I, 93d to 99th percentile) to very low trainability (category V, 9th percentile and lower). The services have found that entrants scoring below the 31st percentile (categories IV and V) require more training and present greater disciplinary problems than those in the higher groups, and those scoring in category V are disqualified. *Test Manual for the Armed Services Vocational Aptitude Battery*, DOD 1304.12AA (North Chicago, Ill.: U.S. Military Entrance Processing Command, July 1984), p. 2.

Figure 3-7. *Black Army Recruits as Share of All Recruits and Share of All Recruits Scoring in Top Half of Population, Fiscal Years 1979–91*

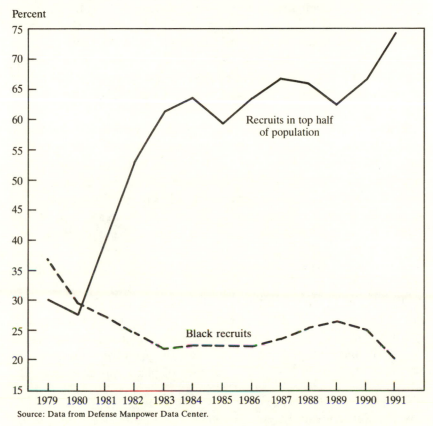

Percent

Source: Data from Defense Manpower Data Center.

70,000 in 1991, the proportion of "choice" recruits increased from 66.6 percent to 74.5 percent, and the proportion of black recruits fell from 25 to 20 percent (figure 3-7).[77]

The services' success in attracting these highly qualified volunteers has varied, depending mostly on supply and demand in the recruiting mar-

77. "Choice" recruits, in the eyes of the services, are high school graduates with above-average aptitudes for military skills. Those who have completed high school are considered more likely to complete their initial obligation, and those with high test scores are considered easier to train. The Army, for example, establishes recruiting goals for this category of volunteers, dubbed GSMAs (seniors or high school graduates who score in the top half of the population of test takers).

ketplace.[78] Since the remarkable easing of recruitment in the early 1980s, the armed forces have drawn an unprecedented proportion of these choice recruits. Compared with 1979, for example, when only 30 percent of all Army recruits scored at or above the 50th percentile, 75 percent in 1991 were in that category. But as the intake of these highly qualified recruits rose steeply in the early 1980s and again in the early 1990s, the proportion of black recruits fell (figure 3-7), in part because of differences in the abilities of white and black youths to meet the choice recruit standard.

Blacks are less likely to have completed high school and far less likely to score among the top half of recruits on the standardized entry test. A nationwide administration of the entry test in 1980, for example, indicated that only 14 percent of black men can be expected to score in the top half of the population compared with 61 percent of white men. The mean score attained by blacks was 24.29 compared with 55.97 for whites, a difference of more than one standard deviation of the total population's score distribution.[79]

ARE BLACKS LOSING INTEREST? Although much of the recent drop in black recruitment can be attributed to changes in entry standards, black youths also seem less interested in military service than they were in the 1980s. The proportion with a "positive propensity" for military service, which has traditionally been much higher than for whites, has decreased since 1986 and, following a brief recovery, dropped from 53 percent in 1989 to 37 percent in 1992.[80] The number of black applicants also fell,

78. For an excellent discussion of service entry standards and their sensitivity to external factors, see Mark J. Eitelberg and others, *Screening for Service: Aptitude and Education Criteria for Military Entry* (Office of the Assistant Secretary of Defense for Manpower, Installations, and Logistics, September 1984).

79. Office of the Assistant Secretary of Defense for Manpower, Reserve Affairs, and Logistics, *Profile of American Youth: 1980 Nationwide Administration of the Armed Forces Vocational Aptitude Battery* (Department of Defense, March 1982), pp. 24, 77. A spread of one standard deviation means a cutoff score that included the top 50 percent of whites would include only 16 percent of blacks. This is based on the assumption that the scores of blacks and whites are distributed normally and that the standard deviations of each distribution are the same.

80. "Propensity," the inclination to consider military service, has been measured since 1975 by the Youth Attitude Tracking Study (YATS), sponsored by the Department of Defense. The study gathers information about the characteristics, values, aspirations, and activities of young people in the military's traditional recruitment target population. For a description of the methodology, see Peter F. Ramsberger, "Characteristics of Youth and Propensity for Military Service: Findings from the 1990 Communications and Enlistment

from 120,000 in 1989, when they constituted 23 percent of all applicants, to about 66,000 in 1991, or less than 17 percent of the total.

It is premature to draw conclusions because the decreasing black interest has not been fully analyzed, but the decrease may have been prompted by the Persian Gulf conflict and the realization by youths and their parents that military service is more than just a peacetime job opportunity. This realization would have been strengthened by the general disaffection among the African American population for U.S. military involvement in the Gulf in the first place and the concerns about casualties expressed by many black leaders as the buildup progressed. Many young blacks also may have become discouraged and dropped out of the pool of prospective volunteers as enlistment prospects diminished sharply during the 1980s.[81]

In any event, if trends observed during the initial phases of the force reduction are any indication, the racial mix of the Army will become more representative of the population. A decreasing proportion of black recruits can be expected to continue if the services persist in emphasizing the importance of entry test scores and if the number of highly qualified blacks seeking to volunteer for military service shrinks.

The effect of personnel reductions on the composition of the career force is more difficult to predict. In the short run, much will depend on the specific plans, especially on how each category of personnel is affected. This has been a source of controversy as the various services have made different assessments of the trade-offs among the ways to trim the career force: accept fewer entrants into the career force by reducing reenlistment opportunities; induce those already in the career force to separate; or encourage those who are eligible to retire. Under any circumstance, the impact would likely be small for the Army because blacks make up such a large proportion of careerists, and particularly because the effects would be transitional.

Once the size of the Army stabilizes, the composition of the career force over the longer term would be influenced by the occupational char-

---

Decisions/Youth Attitude Tracking Study," FR-PRD-91-15, Human Resources Research Organization, Alexandria, Va., October 1991, app. A.

81. This has been apparent in survey data. In 1992, for example, 36 percent of 16- to 21-year-old male respondents indicated they would be "less likely to enlist" in response to the question, "With the budget cuts in the Defense Department, the military may not recruit as many new people as before. How does this affect your attitude towards enlistment?" Data from Department of Defense in Defense Manpower Data Center, "1992 Youth Attitude Tracking Study," memorandum, n.d.

acteristics of the smaller force. For instance, blacks have been overrepresented in health and clerical positions and underrepresented in technical
occupations. If the combat-to-support ratio in the future force is smaller
(perhaps because fewer forward-based forces would decrease logistics
requirements) or if the forces require a greater concentration of technicians (because of more emphasis on technology), the percentage of
blacks in the career force could be expected to decrease. The Army,
however, does not anticipate major changes in its occupational structure.
It has indicated that even though the enlisted force will decrease by 30
percent between 1991 and 1995, support positions will be cut 28 percent.[82]

By all indications, then, any change in the racial composition of the
Army will be gradual and will probably not create undue concern, especially since overrepresentation was an issue raised by many black leaders during the Persian Gulf conflict.

Potential Challenges

In the event of a larger or more abrupt decrease in black participation
in the armed services, however, legislators and interest groups could be
expected to intervene to prevent any significant erosion of job opportunities for African American youth.

The most obvious means for protecting military job opportunities for
blacks would be to provide affirmative action "guidance" or to set goals
or objectives similar to those used by the services in the past to ensure
equity on military promotion boards. This approach could prove difficult,
however, because it would certainly evoke images of quotas—a code word
with distasteful political overtones.

Besides, the Pentagon probably has little choice but to maintain what
it has proudly called, since the advent of the all-volunteer force, a color-
blind recruitment policy. To do otherwise now would fly in the face of the
principle established during the early years of the all-volunteer force,
when Army Secretary Clifford Alexander answered critics of the growing
racial imbalance by contending that the number of blacks in the Army
was "immaterial": "Who is going to play God and set a quota?"[83]

82. Bernard Adelsberger, "Drawdown May Tip Racial Scales," *Army Times*, December
23, 1991, p. 45.
83. David Binder, "Army Head Favors Volunteers," *New York Times*, February 11, 1977,
p. A14.

There are, however, other ways to "regulate" the racial balance of the armed forces. Entry standards are instrumental in determining the racial composition, and observers concerned with protecting black volunteers during the troop reductions could question whether the standards are valid predictors of performance and the entry test itself free of racial bias. Moreover, it would be fair to ask whether the services might be seeking volunteers with levels of education and test scores higher than are necessary.

The armed services have screened potential recruits with standardized tests since World War I. Used initially to identify the mentally unfit, in recent years the tests have been used to assess vocational aptitude. The services have placed great stock in them because research has shown that people with higher aptitude scores are more trainable—they complete skill training courses at a higher rate than low scorers, complete them sooner, get higher grades, and retain the information longer. Also, research has verified a close connection between entry aptitude and skill qualification test scores and rates of promotion.

At the same time, standardized tests have been heavily criticized as to how accurately they measure aptitude, achievement, or intelligence and whether they are truly divorced from the influences of education and environment. Such tests, it has been argued, also fail to measure idealism, stamina, persistence, and creativity, which to many observers are as important as cognitive skills. The primary charge, however, is that standardized tests do not measure the same dimensions of achievement across different groups.

In the early 1980s the Army itself questioned the validity of the tests. In response to a growing intolerance in Congress of the increase in low-scoring, mainly black, recruits, an ad hoc study group in the Army secretariat examined the validity of standardized tests and reported, "The Army cautiously states that results of the AFQT [Armed Forces Qualification Test] indicate, at best, trainability. The evidence we have gathered, however, suggests that the test has been so misrepresented over time, and the predictions derived from Mental Category results so overstated, that the future utility of the AFQT is in some doubt."[84]

84. "An Examination of the Use of the Armed Forces Qualification Test (AFQT) as a Screen and a Measure of Quality," report to the Secretary of the Army and the Chief of Staff (Department of the Army, July 1980), p. iii. This study, known as the Lister report after Army General Counsel Sara E. Lister, was carried out during Secretary of the Army

The study group further argued that "linking Mental Category with job performance is not only inaccurate but against the best interests of manpower management in the Army—which requires finding the soldier who can do the job." To this end the group suggested that the Army convert from a norm-referenced system, which compares one candidate with others, to a criterion-referenced system, which compares a candidate with a describably constant standard of performance.[85] Prompted in part by this controversy, the Joint-Service Job Performance Measurement/ Enlistment Standards (JPM) Project was established by the Pentagon in 1980 to develop "measures of performance in entry-level military jobs so that, for the first time, military enlistment standards could be linked to performance on the job."[86]

After more than a decade of research, a technical committee of the National Academy of Sciences concluded that "the JPM Project provided ample evidence that ASVAB scores are related to job proficiency," but found a "somewhat higher correlation between the entrance tests and the job knowledge performance measure than between the entrance tests and hands-on measures." This result, not unanticipated, was particularly evident among minorities. Compared with a difference of 0.85 standard deviation between whites and blacks on the entry test and 0.78 on the job knowledge test, both of which are paper-and-pencil, multiple-choice tests, the difference narrowed to 0.36 on the hands-on test, leading the researchers to conclude that "to the extent that we have confidence in the hands-on criterion as a good measure of performance on the job, these findings strongly suggest that scores on the ASVAB exaggerate the size of the differences that will ultimately be found in the job performance of the two groups."[87]

This suggests the possibility that the wide differences in predicted performance between blacks and whites implied by entry test scores are significantly narrowed as recruits gain on-the-job experience. The implications of these findings were skirted by the committee, which indicated

---

Clifford Alexander's term. It is no secret that the military leadership was at odds with the secretary on many issues, including this one.

85. "Examination of Use of Armed Forces Qualification Test," pp. III-11, IV-6. For a discussion of criterion-referenced systems, see W. James Popham, *Criterion-Referenced Measurement* (Prentice-Hall, 1978).

86. Alexandra K. Wigdor and Bert F. Green, Jr., eds., *Performance Assessment for the Workplace* (Washington: National Academy Press, 1991), p. vii.

87. Wigdor and Green, eds., *Performance Assessment*, pp. 11, 179.

that "this issue goes well beyond the JPM Project; it calls for the attention of the measurement profession as a whole."[88]

The Army, meanwhile, established its own elaborate research effort designed to develop new measures of job performance, validate existing selection measures, develop and validate new selection and classification measures, develop a scale to improve job classification decisions, and estimate the relative usefulness and validity of alternative selection and classification procedures. Among its many research objectives, the study was to "determine the extent of differential prediction across racial and gender groups for a systematic sample of individual differences, performance factors, and jobs." As of 1990, however, work on the jobs objective was described as "ongoing."[89]

It is also possible, if opportunities for blacks are substantially diminished, that the military's entry test will be scrutinized for racial bias. This question, too, had been raised in the Army's 1980 Lister report, which contended that certain words included in the test "will disproportionately reflect a cultural background typical of the majority male population of white test-takers."[90] The problem was not pursued, however, because blacks were passing the test and entering the Army in record numbers. In any case, there have been few charges of cultural bias in military testing, which is somewhat surprising since standardized tests in nonmilitary settings have been subjected to growing criticism.[91]

Nevertheless, studies conducted by the Air Force have indicated that the test meets appropriate federal standards and the equations for predicting training performance are essentially the same for whites and minorities and for men and women. In fact, where differences were ob-

88. Wigdor and Green, eds., *Performance Assessment*, p. 179.

89. John P. Campbell, "An Overview of the Army Selection and Classification Project (Project A)," *Personnel Psychology*, vol. 43 (Summer 1990), pp. 232–33. This seven-year research effort initiated in 1983 was conducted by the Army Research Institute for the Behavioral and Social Sciences and a consortium of three research firms. The summer 1990 issue of *Personnel Psychology* is devoted to a description of the project and summarizes its findings.

90. "Examination of the Use of the Armed Forces Qualification Test," p. III-30. Bias in testing is a complex, highly technical question on which it is difficult to obtain a consensus, even about its meaning. For an overview of the literature, see Mark J. Eitelberg, "Subpopulation Differences in Performance on Tests of Mental Ability: Historical Review and Annotated Bibliography," technical memorandum 81–3 (Directorate for Accession Policy, Office of the Secretary of Defense, August 1981).

91. For a general discussion of cultural bias in standardized testing, see Robert L. Green and Robert J. Griffore, "The Impact of Standardized Testing on Minority Students," *Journal of Negro Education*, vol. 49 (Summer 1980), pp. 238–52.

served, the predictions for the training school grades of minorities were too optimistic. In other words, the test predicted minority examinees would do better in training than they actually did.[92]

Finally, in a technical assessment of the test battery, the National Opinion Research Center found that responses were "free from major defects such as high levels of guessing or carelessness, inappropriate levels of difficulty, cultural test-question bias, and inconsistencies in test administration procedures." The investigators therefore concluded that the test results "provide a sound basis for the estimation of population attributes such as means, medians, and percentile points, for the youth population as a whole and for subpopulations defined by age, sex, and race/ethnicity."[93]

Considering such findings, the Pentagon's general counsel concluded in 1977 that the ASVAB met the Fifth Amendment due process standard, which requires that "no discriminatory purpose be present and requires proof only that the test predicts performance in a training course." Title VII of the Civil Rights Act of 1964, however, sets a stricter standard, requiring proof that a test predicts performance on the job. The Office of the General Counsel concluded that under its interpretation, Title VII "does not apply to members of the armed forces. If the Court disagrees and applies Title VII standards to the ASVAB test, we would not be able at this point to prove that the test is related to job performance."[94]

Admittedly, it is difficult to envision Pentagon decisionmakers or legislators debating the esoteric psychometric problems of standards validation and test bias. More conceivable, however, is the prospect that fiscally minded legislators or the Pentagon's civilian leaders could ask, how much quality is enough? Because the marginal costs—incentives, advertising expenses, number of recruiters, and the like—to attract and

92. Nancy Guinn, Ernest C. Tupes, and William E. Allen, "Cultural Subgroup Differences in the Relationships between Air Force Aptitude Composites and Training Criteria" (Lackland Air Force Base, Tex.: Air Force Human Resources Laboratory, September 1970). See also Lonnie D. Valentine, "Prediction of Air Force Technical Training Success from ASVAB and Educational Background," Lackland Air Force Base, Tex.: Air Force Human Resources Laboratory, May 1977.

93. R. Darrell Bock and Robert J. Mislevy, "The Profile of American Youth: Data Quality Analysis of the Armed Services Vocational Aptitude Battery," University of Chicago, National Opinion Research Center, August 1981, p. 51.

94. Department of Defense, Office of the General Counsel, "Does the ASVAB Test Meet Applicable Legal Requirements Prohibiting Use of Tests That Discriminate on the Basis of Race, Color, Religion, Sex or National Origin?" Memorandum, September 1977, p. 6.

retain high-quality volunteers are higher, the services, especially the Army, might be put under greater pressure to defend their higher standards.

Clearly, every job in the armed forces does not need to be filled by people with above-average scores on the military entrance test, and it is reasonable to ask the services to specify the relation between test results and job performance. During the transition to an all-volunteer force, the Pentagon's civilian leadership acknowledged that too much quality could be counterproductive: "Overall, the learning capacity of new entries is adequate in meeting job requirements when the proportion of Mental Group IV personnel does not exceed about 22 percent. Conversely, when the overall proportion of Mental Group IV personnel falls below 15 percent, there is a tendency toward many people being under-challenged by their job assignments."[95]

The Army was more specific in a report to Congress in 1985, presenting a distribution of recruit test scores that "would be both cost effective and sufficient to support the Army's force structure and manpower requirements" (the actual 1991 mix is shown for comparison):[96]

Test score category	"Cost-effective" mix (percent)	FY 1991 mix (percent)
I-IIIA (GSMA)	59–63	74.5
IIIB	31–27	24.4
IV	10	1.0

It would thus appear that the Army is recruiting higher quality personnel than it recently considered cost effective, which suggests there is substantial leeway for adjusting entry standards without compromising military effectiveness.

A Hobson's Choice

It is easy to understand why the delicate issue of racial representation in the armed forces has gone largely unaddressed. Many observers, after

95. "The All-Volunteer Force and the End of the Draft," special report of Secretary of Defense Elliot L. Richardson (March 1973), p. 13, as quoted in Martin Binkin and John D. Johnston, *All-Volunteer Armed Forces: Progress, Problems, and Prospects*, Committee Print, Senate Committee on Armed Services, 93 Cong. 1 sess. (GPO, June 1973), p. 52.

96. Office of the Assistant Secretary of Defense for Manpower, Installations, and Logistics, *Defense Manpower Quality*, vol. 2: *Army Submission* (Department of Defense, May 1985), p. xii. Fiscal year 1991 data are from Defense Manpower Data Center.

all, deny the existence of a problem, contending that today's volunteers, black or white, are merely exercising their freedom of choice. Any suggestions that the volunteers might be economic conscripts or might be making uninformed decisions are dismissed as condescending. Besides, some would ask, is the alternative—unemployment—better? Other observers contend that the current distribution is about right and are confident that it would require a war bigger than anything foreseeable to impose truly disproportionate casualties on African Americans. Besides, as the Vietnam experience indicated, actions can and probably would be taken to hold casualty rates closer to the general population norms than to the composition of the force. To this group, the racial composition of the armed forces is not at issue.

Other Americans who, for a variety of reasons, harbor concerns about or are uncomfortable with fielding a racially unbalanced military force and would prefer a more representative force confront a Hobson's choice. Some are resigned to the fact that young African Americans are entering into a devil's bargain, made necessary by a society that has failed to provide them with the tools needed to compete in the nonmilitary marketplace. Their solution is social reform aimed at upgrading the status and skills of the underprivileged and redressing the disparities that make the armed forces the most attractive—and often the only—employment opportunity available to them. But the observers recognize that even the most successful programs would take years to undo what decades of social and educational neglect have created. In the meantime they would not limit the opportunities that blacks now enjoy in the armed forces. Some would even preserve the proportion at the current high levels.

Others, pointing to the inequities of a racially unbalanced military that became obvious during the Persian Gulf conflict, are unwilling to wait for social reforms. They would have the nation return to conscription or adopt policies that would yield a more representative force, neither of which, at this juncture, would appear to be socially or politically acceptable, much less accomplish the intended purpose.

The inescapable conclusion, then, is that the nation will field a racially unrepresentative force until it can resolve the many complex problems that contribute to the greater propensity among blacks for military service. It seems safe to speculate, however, that if the changes since the end of the Persian Gulf conflict become a trend, blacks' overrepresentation in the Army will diminish. The pace of change will depend largely on how free the Army is to emphasize manpower quality as it shrinks. It would be wrongheaded to preclude the Army from pursuing that goal just to preserve a given racial composition. But it would be equally improper to permit it to do so without closely scrutinizing its standards and test instruments and the rationale underlying them.

If nothing else, the Persian Gulf experience has provided the nation with a better understanding of the racial composition of its armed forces and its implications. Perhaps the public's awareness that a higher percentage of African Americans than whites is in peril in time of war will foster awareness that a higher percentage is also in economic peril in time of peace.

CHAPTER FOUR

What Role for the Weekend Warriors?

CITIZEN-SOLDIERING, with roots in the militia concept of the seventeenth century, has been a part of the American culture since the founding of the Republic. The nation's contemporary military reserve forces, however, bear little resemblance to their antecedents in their size, organization, or character.[1]

The modern reserve concept was shaped after World War II as the United States, fearful of the spread of communism in general and the Sino-Soviet military threat in particular, fielded the largest peacetime military forces in its history. During the early stages of the cold war, the reserves were considered backups to be called on to augment the active forces in extreme national emergencies, a concept that was given its first test at the outbreak of the Korean War. Their role was modified during the 1960s as "partial mobilizations" became instruments of diplomacy rather than tools of military necessity. Small numbers of reservists were mobilized briefly during the Berlin crisis in 1961 and following the capture of the *USS Pueblo* by the North Koreans and onset of the Tet offensive in Vietnam in early 1968.

The character and composition of the contemporary reserve forces were reshaped again in the early 1970s, as America disengaged from Vietnam and ended its reliance on conscription. The reserves became the primary source for expanding the nation's military forces in an emergency. The term *total force* entered the Pentagon's lexicon, introducing a

1. The terms *reserves* and *reserve forces* are used interchangeably to mean all the reserve units and reservists under the purview of a military service, for example, both the Army Reserve and Army National Guard. When the term is capitalized, as in Army Reserve, the reference is to that specific component alone.

concept under which the reserve components were to fulfill new missions and enjoy higher priorities in military planning.

Since then, the reserves have been increasingly important in national security planning, assigned many responsibilities that traditionally were the preserve of active forces. The effects were most clearly evident in the Army. By the end of the 1980s, reservists comprised half of all trained Army personnel. Many units had been earmarked for deployment along with their active counterparts, some with only a few days' notice and most of the remainder within weeks rather than months or years as before.

Although the fortunes of the reserves have ebbed and flowed under the total force policy, the dominant influence on the policy has been the perceived need to maintain military capabilities larger than the active forces could reasonably be expected to provide to counter the Soviet threat. As that threat has faded, however, so too has the rationale for the size and composition of American military forces in general and of their reserve components in particular. The U.S. military, now adapting to deal with a post–cold war world order, is shrinking and is adjusting its structures and missions to new national security realities. But how the reserves, having participated extensively and successfully in the Persian Gulf conflict, should fit into the new security arrangement has engendered intense debate.

The Reserves and the Cold War

To appreciate fully the possible roles of the reserves, it is important to understand the factors that have shaped the size and structure of the reserves in the past. In the aftermath of World War II, the reserve forces were all but forgotten by the architects of the postwar military establishment who were preoccupied with salvaging a standing force out of the largest and most rapid troop reduction in the nation's history. This was a tall order in the face of an efficiency-minded president, Harry S Truman, and a parsimonious Congress, both of which discounted the prospects of an immediate military confrontation. Amidst the postwar euphoria and given America's nuclear superiority, there was little interest in maintaining a big conventional military capability in the active forces, much less in the reserves. The reserves were looked upon mainly as a pool of experienced troops that could be used to train, organize, and equip the large number of citizen soldiers that would be called again in the unlikely event of another massive mobilization. This disregard of conventional military forces was to exact a toll sooner than expected.

The Korean Conflict

The outbreak of hostilities on the Korean peninsula in June 1950 caught the 1.5 million U.S. armed troops unprepared to engage in a major land campaign. The standing Army especially, consisting of only ten divisions and fewer than 600,000 troops, fell far short of the strength General Douglas MacArthur considered necessary to counter the Communist invasion. Because additional forces were needed far sooner than could be produced through drafting and training new recruits, the Army turned to its citizen-soldiers, many with World War II experience but few with up-to-date training. Although this was far from a complete mobilization, reservists accounted for 35 percent of the buildup that occurred in the first year of the Korean conflict. This experience introduced two new concepts into national security planning—*limited war* and *partial mobilization*—and laid to rest the idea that a major war between the superpowers was the only contingency for which it made sense to plan.

Following the Korean War, the concept of full reserve mobilization was rendered even less relevant as the nation adopted a strategy of massive retaliation. Most people believed that the United States, which enjoyed nuclear superiority, could not get involved in a *protracted* conventional war. The military focused on forces already in existence. If the reserves were to play any part at all, they would need to be able to respond rapidly in a crisis. This rapid response was further emphasized when the Kennedy administration, acknowledging nuclear parity, replaced the strategy of massive retaliation with "flexible response" and initiated a program to upgrade U.S. conventional forces, including the reserve components.

The Berlin Crisis

It did not take long for the revitalized concept of conventional forces to be tested. When U.S.-Soviet relations neared a flash point over the status of Berlin in 1961, President John Kennedy ordered a partial mobilization of the reserves, one of a package of initiatives to convince the Soviet leadership that he was committed to protect American interests in the region. This action constituted the first use of the reserve forces as an instrument of diplomacy, a demonstration of national resolve intended to prevent a war rather than fight one.

But lack of readiness and widespread discontent among recalled reservists resulted in a flurry of congressional protests, shaking the confidence of Secretary of Defense Robert McNamara, who concluded that the reserve system "seemingly was not as available an instrument for emergencies as . . . [he] had hoped. For crises of a scale that did not require a major mobilization, an alternative would have to be found."[2]

The Vietnam War

The Korean and Berlin mobilizations prompted questions about the commitment and the readiness of the reserves. Controversy during the early years of the growing U.S. involvement in Vietnam focused on *nonmobilization*: the administration's failure to use reserves in a situation for which they seemed tailor made. In early 1965, following a series of defeats suffered by the army of South Vietnam, Secretary McNamara proposed that the number of U.S. troops be increased from 75,000 to 175,000, holding out the possibility that an additional 100,000 might be needed in early 1966. To meet these needs, he proposed to call up 235,000 reservists.[3] Although this recommendation was backed by the military leadership and most of President Johnson's close advisers, Johnson chose instead to support the buildup through a larger draft.

This decision, which was to haunt the reserves for years after the Vietnam War, became the subject of widespread disagreement among social commentators and scholars. Some contended the reserves were not prepared. Others pointed to fears that a mobilization might bring China or the Soviet Union into the conflict. An officially sanctioned history of the Army Reserve, however, concluded that "the best historical judgment of the decision not to employ Reserve Component units . . . in Vietnam is that Johnson had made an almost purely political decision."[4] As David Halberstram commented, Johnson "was not about to call up the reserves,

2. William W. Kaufmann, *The McNamara Strategy* (Harper and Row, 1964), p. 71.

3. Martin Binkin and William W. Kaufmann, *U.S. Army Guard and Reserve: Rhetoric, Realities, Risks* (Brookings, 1989), p. 48.

4. Richard B. Crossland and James T. Currie, *Twice the Citizen: A History of the United States Army Reserve, 1908-1983* (Washington: Office of the Chief, Army Reserve, 1984), p. 195.

because . . . it would be self-evident that we were really going to war, and that in fact we would have to pay a price. Which went against all the Administration planning: this would be a war without a price, a silent, politically invisible war."[5]

The controversy over mobilization continued through 1966 and 1967 as the U.S. military commitment in Southeast Asia burgeoned: by the end of 1967, 485,000 troops were in Vietnam.[6] The Joint Chiefs continued to advocate calling up reserves, especially since the war was draining resources from other military commitments. But the administration ignored them, seemingly for the same reasons that underlay the 1965 decision. If anything, "it became even more politically difficult to consider a Reserve call-up, because the Reserve components had become havens for those who wanted to avoid active military duty—and Vietnam."[7] The possibility of mobilization, it should be noted, was not just a sidebar in the story. A well-informed insider at the time later concluded that this constraint on the use of reserves, "with all its political and social repercussions, not any argument about strategic concepts or the 'philosophy' of war, dictated American war policy."[8]

Two events in January 1968—the capture of the *USS Pueblo* by North Korea and the beginning of the Tet offensive in Vietnam—allowed proponents of reserve mobilization to prevail. Even then, however, only a few reservists were activated, an indication that the call-up, like the 1961 activations, was more a signal of national resolve than a necessary augmentation of military strength.

And again, as in the 1961 experience, the results were less than satisfying. The January call-up of Navy and Air Force units was accompanied by press reports critical of the preparedness of the reservists. The reports were followed by widespread news coverage of complaints among mobilized reservists, some of whom charged they were given little to do, while others objected to being used as fillers in active units, rather than serving in their original units with their buddies. Moreover, the influence of domestic politics was much in evidence: considerations of readiness gave way to concerns that recalled units should be geographically representative (seventy-six Army reserve units represented thirty-four states)

5. David Halberstam, *The Best and the Brightest* (Random House, 1972), p. 593.
6. Binkin and Kaufmann, *U.S. Army Guard and Reserve*, p. 52.
7. Crossland and Currie, *Twice the Citizen*, p. 197.
8. Herbert Y. Schandler, *The Unmaking of a President: Lyndon Johnson and Vietnam* (Princeton University Press, 1977), p. 56.

and that the contributions by the National Guard and Reserve components should be proportional. As a result, some units selected for call-up had fewer personnel and were less well equipped than similar units that were not mobilized.[9]

The causes of these problems were not laid entirely at the doorstep of the reserve components. The Army was criticized for its lack of preparedness, inadequate planning, and poor execution, even though it had been given strong signals that the reserves would not be called up. In addition, the tensions that have traditionally marked the relationship of active duty personnel and reserves ran particularly high as the reserve components became havens for those wishing to avoid the draft and probable service in Vietnam. Thanks to conscription, the reserves enjoyed a seemingly endless queue of applicants whose educational attainment and aptitude test scores were much higher than those in the active forces.[10]

These bright, educated reservists, however, represented little military capability—most were merely "counting the days." But even motivated members found it hard to qualify in their designated skills because their units had been stripped of essential equipment and usable training facilities. By the end of the 1970's the war fighting abilities of the reserves, especially the Army's, were considered virtually nonexistent.

It is ironic, then, that as the nation began to disengage from military involvement in Southeast Asia and to fashion its post-Vietnam military, the reserve forces, tarnished image and all, figured prominently. The Nixon administration's launching of the total force concept in 1970 ushered in a reserve renaissance of sorts, leading to a military force structure distinctly different from its recent predecessors and conspicuous for its heavy and early dependence on reserves.

The Total Force Policy

The increased reliance on reserve forces was explained in 1970 by Secretary of Defense Melvin Laird, the architect of the total force policy.

9. John D. Stuckey and Joseph H. Pistorius, "Mobilization for the Vietnam War: A Political and Military Catastrophe," *Parameters*, vol. 15 (Spring 1985), p. 34.

10. This situation was recalled during the 1988 presidential campaign when questions were raised about the seeming incongruity between vice presidential nominee Dan Quayle's standing as a conservative hawk and his enlistment in the Indiana National Guard during the Vietnam War.

Emphasis will be given to concurrent consideration of the total forces, active and reserve, to determine the most advantageous mix to support national strategy and meet the threat. A total force concept will be applied in all aspects of planning, programming, manning, equipping and employing the Guard and Reserve Forces. . . . [These forces] will be prepared to be the initial and primary source for augmentation of the active forces in any future emergency requiring a rapid and substantial expansion of the active forces.[11]

The military services were affected differently. The Air National Guard and the Air Force Reserve, which together accounted for about 1,300 units (squadron size or smaller), had emerged from the Vietnam era with their images intact and were little affected by the new policy. The Air National Guard was involved mainly in air defense and tactical missions, including close air support, interdiction, and airlift. The Air Force Reserve was largely an airlift organization, composed partly of units that had their own aircraft and partly of associate squadrons whose reserve crews flew aircraft assigned to regular Air Force units. The Marine Corps Reserve was also largely unaffected by the new policy. Consisting simply of a fully structured marine amphibious force that, for all practical purposes, was identical to its three active counterparts, the prestige of this component survived the Vietnam conflict even though it was not called on to participate. The Naval Reserve had been geared mainly to providing trained reservists for active-duty ships, which were typically manned in peacetime with fewer people than in wartime. Only 20 percent of naval reservists were in ship or aircraft units, the most prominent of which were two carrier attack wings and thirty-five destroyer-type ships. Naval reserve units, it should be noted, depend heavily on active-duty participation; reservists typically account for only one-third of the company on a reserve ship.

The reserve components most affected by the total force proclamation were the Army Guard and Army Reserve, both of which had languished at the hands of a policy that stripped them of equipment, filled them with draft-averse volunteers, and relegated them to second-class status. With all this baggage, then, how did the Army's reserve components become the principal beneficiaries of the total force concept?

First, the end of conscription in 1973 meant the reserves would have to be the primary source of personnel for rapidly expanding the armed

11. Memorandum from Secretary of Defense Melvin R. Laird to the secretaries of the military departments, reprinted in *Congressional Record*, vol. 116, pt. 23 (September 9, 1970), p. 30968.

forces. Moreover, most observers believed at the time—the belief proved accurate—that among the military services, the Army would experience the most trouble with recruiting and would find it difficult to maintain an active force containing more than 800,000 troops. Thus in 1975 when, in light of the perceived growth in Soviet military power, a decision was made to increase the number of Army divisions from thirteen to sixteen without any increase in active-duty personnel, larger responsibilities had to be assigned to reserve components, both to complement the active force's combat strength and to augment its support forces.

One of the most conspicuous features of the total force policy was the roundout concept under which selected Army combat divisions, which nominally consist of three active brigades of 5,000 men each, would instead be composed of two active brigades and one reserve roundout brigade. This arrangement allowed the Army to field more division flags without an increase in active strength. The concept was intended to benefit the reserves through closer planning and training associations with an active counterpart. The reserve unit was to share with its parent unit a priority ranking in resource allocation, enabling it to maintain a similar readiness status and, in theory at least, making it capable of deploying with its parent division.[12]

The Army created five roundout divisions; four were designated primarily for conflict in Europe and according to 1983 contingency plans, some were expected to deploy within thirty days of mobilization.[13] One roundout division, however, had been earmarked for the U.S. Central Command (CENTCOM), with the expectation that its reserve brigade would be ready for deployment shortly after mobilization. Together with the roundout brigades, ten Army National Guard divisions along with separate brigades in the reserve components represented more than 40 percent of the Army's personnel in the combat division forces.

The Army also assigned a wide range of combat support and combat service support functions to its reserve components. By 1989 the reserves

12. In a related concept, called roundup, a reserve unit complements rather than substitutes for an active unit. A National Guard brigade, for example, could be the fourth brigade attached to a fully constituted active division. These units would be expected to undergo more postmobilization training than round-out units and would likely be employed in later stages as combat replacements.

13. An unclassified illustrative deployment sequence for European deployment can be found in Office of the Assistant Secretary of Defense for Program Analysis and Evaluation, *NATO Center Region Military Balance Study, 1978-1984* (Department of Defense, July 1979), annex A.

accounted for 89 percent of maintenance companies, 90 percent of supply and service units, 67 percent of combat engineer units, 67 percent of truck companies, and 68 percent of conventional ammunition companies. Many units, moreover, had been assigned missions in support of forward deployed forces in central Europe, since Congress had placed limits on the ratio of active duty support to combat personnel in that theater.[14] To fulfill those responsibilities, many reserve units would have had to mobilize and deploy in a matter of days, a capability that was not only unprecedented but that warranted skepticism. Nonetheless, the Army deliberately maintained support units that were less than fully ready, accepting the risk in anticipation that they could be made ready in far less time than combat units.[15]

Although the end of conscription greatly influenced this new role for the Army's reserve forces, so too did cost. Secretary Laird set the dollar-and-cents undertone of total force when he inaugurated the concept: "Lower sustaining costs of non-active duty forces . . . allows more force units to be provided for the same cost as an all-active force structure, or the same number of force units to be maintained at lesser cost."[16] Sixteen years later, the House Armed Services Committee still subscribed to that rationale: "The Total Force concept has proven to be an effective method of increasing U.S. national security—and at only 40 to 70 percent of the cost of active duty personnel."[17]

Finally, the closer association between the active Army and its reserve components, it has been held, was fostered by General Creighton Abrams in the wake of the Vietnam experience "to ensure that never again would a President be able to send the Army to war without the reserves maintained for such a contingency." Reestablishing the concept of the citizen-soldier as a bridge between the active Army and the American people, it was believed, would reduce the risk that the Army would be politically

14. The so-called Nunn amendment, attached to the Defense Department Appropriation Authorization Act of 1975, required the Army to cut 18,000 military support positions in Europe during fiscal 1975–76 while permitting the creation of an equal number of combat positions. P.L. 93-365, sec. 302, 88 Stat. 399, 401 (1974).

15. In peacetime, Army support units, on average, are manned at 90 percent of their wartime levels, compared with 97 percent for combat units. See General Accounting Office, *Operation Desert Storm: Army Had Difficulty Providing Adequate Active and Reserve Support Forces* (March 1992), p. 36.

16. Department of Defense, *Fiscal Year 1972–76 Defense Program and the 1972 Defense Budget* (March 9, 1971), p. 36.

17. *National Defense Authorization Act for Fiscal Year 1988/1989*, H. Rept. 100-58, 100 Cong. 1 sess. (GPO, 1987), p. 186.

and socially isolated in a war.[18] "If reserves must be activated in order to sustain active forces in anything more than limited contingencies," according to one interpretation, "presidents will be less inclined (and politically less able) to become involved in military actions without extensive national debate and political consensus."[19]

The Reserve Force Renaissance

Whatever the rationale, the adoption of the total force policy in 1971 ushered in a revitalization that was to span the next two decades. Improvements in manning, equipping, and training reserve units were planned, but many were slow to be realized.

Immediately after the end of conscription, the Army's reserve components could not recruit enough volunteers to maintain the strengths authorized by Congress. This was not entirely unexpected; the reserves were largely unfamiliar with recruiting strategies and lacked a recruiting apparatus, having been beneficiaries of an abundant supply of volunteers seeking to avoid the draft. Nor could they look for help from the active Army, which was grappling with recruiting problems of its own. Personnel levels decreased, and by 1978 the combined strength of the Army National Guard and Army Reserve had dipped below 550,000 (figure 4-1). Though smaller, the reserves could claim that their members were true volunteers who, if not as well educated, bright, or affluent as their draft-induced predecessors, were better motivated.

The readiness of reserve units, meanwhile, remained far below desired standards. The Army, which was struggling within tight budgets to maintain the capabilities of its active troops, continued to equip reserve units with hand-me-down hardware, much of which was obsolete. Few units were able to achieve the Army's standards for combat readiness. And because the reserves had to compete with the active forces for limited

18. Harry G. Summers, Jr., "The Army after Vietnam," in Kenneth J. Hagan and William R. Roberts, eds., *Against All Enemies: Interpretations of American Military History from Colonial Times to the Present* (Westport, Conn.: Greenwood Press, 1986), p. 363. Summers was a member of the Strategic Assessment Group, set up by General Creighton W. Abrams to devise a role for the Army in the post-Vietnam world. For a detailed discussion of General Abrams's participation, see Lewis Sorley, "Creighton Abrams and Active-Reserve Integration in Wartime," *Parameters*, vol. 21 (Summer 1991), pp. 43–46.

19. James L. Lacy, "Whither the All-Volunteer Force?" *Yale Law and Policy Review*, vol. 5 (Fall–Winter 1986), p. 63.

Figure 4-1. *Army Personnel, by Component, Fiscal Years 1973–91*

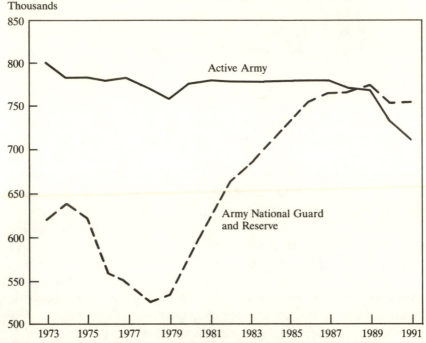

Thousands

Sources: Active Army strengths from Directorate for Information Operations and Reports, Washington Headquarters Services, *Selected Manpower Statistics, Fiscal Year 1991* (Department of Defense, 1990), pp. 60–61; Reserve strengths FY 1973–77 from Office of the Assistant Secretary of Defense for Manpower, Reserve Affairs and Logistics, *Manpower Requirements Report for Fiscal Year 1979* (Department of Defense, 1978), p. ix–14; Reserve strengths FY 1978–87 from Directorate for Information Operations and Reports, Washington Headquarters Services, *Selected Manpower Statistics, Fiscal Year 1987* (Department of Defense, 1986), p. 204; Reserve strengths FY 1988–91 from Office of the Assistant Secretary of Defense for Reserve Affairs, *Official Guard and Reserve Manpower Strengths and Statistics, Fiscal Year 1992 Summary*, RCS:DD-RA(M) 1147/1148, p. 2.001.

openings in training courses, many units could not meet minimum training standards. This neglect eventually caught the attention of the reserves' Capitol Hill supporters, who urged the Pentagon to take the total force concept more seriously.

In 1976 Congress reinforced its confidence in the reserves by authorizing the president to mobilize up to 50,000 reservists for ninety days (with an option to extend for an additional ninety days) without declaring a national emergency. Though the measure was designed to facilitate a limited objective—the Air Force's need to augment its strategic transport capabilities in an emergency—the legislation covered all units in the Selected Reserve.[20] Some of the measure's proponents believed it would

20. The Selected Reserve, the largest reserve category, is composed almost exclusively

serve another purpose: to convince the leaders of the active military that the reserves were an asset that could be safely included in contingency planning. This legislation was a significant departure from previous policy, and many observers were surprised that Congress was willing to sacrifice even this limited measure of warmaking authority.

Despite the ambitious pronouncements that accompanied the establishment of the total force and congressional actions to provide more resources, the Army's reserve components in 1980 were little better than they had been in 1970. Their problems mirrored many of those that plagued the "hollow" active Army of the 1970s, which was not only beset by budgetary problems but was being filled with the most poorly educated and least trainable recruits in recent memory.

The fortunes of the military brightened in 1981 with the inauguration of Ronald Reagan, who launched the largest and most rapid peacetime defense buildup in the nation's history. The Army, with the encouragement of the incoming civilian leadership, sought to add 100,000 active troops by 1987, but indicated that to achieve this growth would "require *extraordinary manpower policies* to include significant augmentation to the Volunteer Concept."[21] Because "extraordinary manpower policies" surely meant conscription, which was anathema to the Reagan administration, Secretary Caspar Weinberger was reportedly livid.[22] The Army revised its strategy, deciding to forgo personnel increases and choosing instead to concentrate on weapons modernization and readiness programs.

In 1984, repeating its actions of the mid-1970s, the Army increased the number of active divisions (this time from sixteen to eighteen) without adding to its active strength. The action necessitated expanding the roundout concept. By fiscal year 1989, six of the eighteen active divisions included a reserve roundout brigade, and three others relied on one or

---

of organized reserve units. All of its members drill periodically and are paid. Its strength is authorized annually by Congress. The legislation also specified that reserve units could be called to active duty only for "operational missions." These limitations, and their varying interpretations, would exact a toll during the mobilization for the Persian Gulf conflict in 1990.

21. Jeanne Holm, *Women in the Military: An Unfinished Revolution*, rev. ed. (Novato, Calif.: Presidio Press, 1992), p. 395.

22. Holm, *Women in the Military*, p. 395. In hindsight, given the dramatically improved recruitment climate during the 1980s, the Army probably could have increased its strength without resorting to conscription. Had it done so, however, it would have faced even more formidable problems adjusting to the post–cold war reductions in the 1990s.

more reserve roundout battalions.[23] Army National Guard divisions were increased from eight to ten during the period.

The Army's reserve components grew dramatically in the 1980s as they adopted more vigorous recruiting programs, supported by large increases in pay and better educational benefits. Increased funding also enabled the Army reserves, especially the National Guard component, to make marked improvements in readiness. And starting in 1982, Congress established separate appropriations, in addition to those included in the Army budget, specifically for reserve procurement. By 1988 more than $2 billion had been appropriated for reserve equipment, mainly tracked and wheeled vehicles and communications equipment. Meanwhile the Army began issuing some of its latest high-technology weapons systems to the reserves, including M1 tanks and Bradley fighting vehicles. The first recipients were those roundout units with the earliest deployment commitments. By 1987, four National Guard tank battalions were equipped with factory-fresh M1s and four others with updated M60A3 tanks. The Army also announced plans to field the AH-64 Apache attack helicopter with Guard units in fiscal year 1988.[24]

Congress, meanwhile, had given the president even greater leeway to use the reserves by amending the authority granted in 1976. In 1980, largely to emphasize the importance of the rapid deployment force set up under President Carter's Persian Gulf doctrine, it doubled to 100,000 the number of reservists that could be mobilized without declaration of a national emergency. Legislation in 1986 doubled the number again, this time in recognition of the wider and earlier role assigned to the reserves.[25]

By the end of the 1980s the Army's reserve components, while still reporting some shortages of skilled personnel and equipment, were unquestionably better than their Vietnam-era predecessors and perhaps in the highest state of readiness in their history. The Army, too, was now configured so that it could conduct only the smallest military operations without involving the reserves.

Some observers nevertheless continued to question the wisdom of the total force policy, contending that too much was expected of part-time

23. *Department of Defense Annual Report to the Congress, Fiscal Year 1990*, p. 128.
24. *Annual Report of the Reserve Forces Policy Board, Fiscal Year 1986*, p. 52.
25. P.L. 99-661; reprinted in *National Defense Authorization Act for Fiscal Year 1987*, H. Rept. 99-1001, 99 Cong. 2 sess. (GPO, 1986), p. 57. This legislation also gave the president authority to extend the period of service to 180 days if he deemed it necessary in the interests of national security.

soldiers. Some important questions were raised: Could the reserve units fulfill their new responsibilities, especially those for which early deployment was a necessity? Could Georgia's 48th Infantry Brigade, for example, which rounded out the 24th Infantry Division, move out as early as its rapid deployment mission might require? If so, would it be able to accomplish its combat mission? How ready were the many Army Reserve combat and support units earmarked for deployment to Europe within a few days of a decision to mobilize? Could they actually provide the support needed to sustain forces engaged in combat? Would the National Guard divisions slated to reinforce NATO several weeks after mobilization be ready in time?[26] The answers were far from clear. According to James Webb, then assistant secretary of defense for reserve affairs, the expanded reliance on the reserves constituted a "serious gamble."[27]

Meanwhile, Congress began to chide the Pentagon for not having used the liberal call-up authority granted in the 1976 legislation. The opportunities for invoking the measure, argued one naval analyst, had presented themselves on numerous occasions. "Between 1976 and 1984, U.S. Navy and Marine forces alone responded to 41 incidents or crises . . . with an average duration of response in some geographic areas in excess of 100 days. . . . In each case, active naval forces were stretched, deployments were altered and/or extended, exercises were cancelled, leaves were cancelled or delayed, but no reserves were [involuntarily] activated."[28]

A seemingly ideal situation for the administration to use its new call-up authority, if only to demonstrate its willingness to do so, occurred in September 1987 when six naval reserve minesweepers were deployed to the Persian Gulf to escort Kuwaiti oil tankers that had been reflagged to discourage Iran from attacking them. Naval reserve crewmembers, who accounted for one-third of each ship's company, however, were not mobilized. Although some of the reservists were permitted to volunteer for the deployment, active duty sailors were taken from other duties to fill

26. Binkin and Kaufmann, *U.S. Army Guard and Reserve*, p. 91.
27. James H. Webb, Jr., "Why U.S. National Guardsmen Train in Honduras," *New York Times*, October 7, 1986, p. A30.
28. James L. Lacy, *Naval Reserve Forces: The Historical Experience with Involuntary Recalls*, research memorandum 86-76 (Alexandria, Va.: Center for Naval Analysis, April 1986), p. 19. Reservists had served on active duty during this period (for example, in Grenada), but all were volunteers.

out the crew.[29] Whether the decision not to mobilize the reservists came from the White House or the Pentagon remains unclear, but while the authority granted by Congress made it legally easier for the president to call up the reserves, it did not make it politically easier.

The Post–Cold War Period

Many of the questions that had been raised about extensive reliance on the reserves became moot with the stunning events in late 1989 that brought an end to the cold war. When the Warsaw Pact disintegrated and the Soviet military threat diminished, so too did the importance of planning for a European conflict, which had not only dominated U.S. national security considerations for four decades but had been the raison d'etre of the reserves. As Congress contemplated the implications of an emerging, if not well-defined, new world order for the future of the American military, it directed the Pentagon to review the operation, effectiveness, and soundness of the total force policy, examine the assignment of missions within and between the active and reserve components, and assess the structure of active and reserve forces.[30]

The Total Force Policy Study Group set up by the Pentagon in December 1989 faced a formidable task. Although the group might have been able to address general principles underlying the total force (the relative costs of active and reserve units, for example), it could not be expected to evaluate alternative mixes of active and reserve forces when the administration had not yet formulated a new strategic vision and Pentagon planners had not yet defined new military threats.

In early 1990, in fact, the administration was struggling to develop a new foreign policy and an updated conventional defense strategy. The Pentagon's leadership hinted of new strategic visions and vaguely described a base force plan in congressional testimony and interviews. But the plan, the brainchild of the Undersecretary of Defense for Policy and the Chairman of the Joint Chiefs of Staff, did not enjoy the full support of the military services. General Colin Powell contended that "getting

29. For elaboration, see Martin Binkin, "We Aren't Ready to Test Reserves' Readiness—for Good Reason," *Los Angeles Times*, October 13, 1987, pt. 2, p. 7.

30. Department of Defense, *Total Force Policy Interim Report to the Congress* (September 1990), p. 1.

the chiefs to go along had been like fitting a size-ten foot into a size-eight shoe."[31]

The Total Force Goes to War

The deliberations of the study group were interrupted in August 1990 with President George Bush's proclamation that Iraq's occupation of Kuwait "will not stand," a statement he backed up with the commitment of U.S. military forces to the Persian Gulf. The total force was to face its first real test, and the study group stood to inherit an unexpected source of empirical data. On August 22, 1990, twenty days after Iraq invaded Kuwait, the president authorized the mobilization of up to 48,800 reservists, a force to be composed of no more than 25,000 Army reservists, and 6,300 from the Navy, 3,000 from the Marine Corps, and 14,500 from the Air Force. In the instructions issued on August 24 by Secretary Richard Cheney, the Army was authorized to call up only combat support and combat service support units. The other services were permitted to call up combat units.

The president authorized the call-up under the provision that allowed mobilization without a declaration of national emergency (title 10, section 673b). This is important, because it restricted the call-up to members of the Selected Reserve and limited the term of service to six months.

The mobilization proceeded gradually: 7,000 reservists by the end of August, 26,000 by the end of September, 33,000 by the end of October, and 44,847 by November 18.[32] Most were Army reservists serving in medical, maintenance, terminal operations, military police, and intelligence units, but the forces included two National Guard field artillery brigades, which are classified by the Army as combat support. Naval reservists were principally in medical, logistic support, and Seabee units, while Air Force reservists filled airlift, medical, command and control, and security police billets. On November 14th the ceiling on reserve call-ups was increased to 125,000 and on December 1 to 188,000, remaining within the 200,000 person limit imposed under the authority.

31. Bob Woodward, *The Commanders* (Simon and Schuster, 1991), p. 231.
32. Statement of Stephen M. Duncan, assistant secretary of defense for reserve affairs, in *Department of Defense Authorization for Appropriations for Fiscal Years 1992 and 1993*, Hearings before the Senate Armed Services Committee, 102 Cong. 1 sess. (GPO, 1991), pt. 6, p. 446.

Table 4-1. *Reservists Mobilized for Persian Gulf Conflict, by Category and Service, as of March 10, 1991*

Service	Selected Reserve	Individual Ready Reserve	Total
Army	126,037	13,170	139,207
Navy	19,948	15	19,963
Marine Corps	26,659	6,204	32,863
Air Force	33,792	842	34,634
Total	206,436	20,231	226,667

Source: Statement of Stephen M. Duncan, Assistant Secretary of Defense for Reserve Affairs, in *Department of Defense Authorization for Appropriations for Fiscal Years 1992 and 1993*, Hearings before the Senate Armed Services Committee, 102 Cong. 1 sess. (GPO, 1991), pt. 6, p. 449.

The president could have chosen to use much broader authority to mobilize up to 1 million members of the Ready Reserve, including members of the Individual Ready Reserve, for up to two years.[33] This would have required reliance on a declaration of a national emergency, which in fact had been made on August 2, 1990, to freeze assets held in the United States by the Iraqi and Kuwaiti governments.[34] But the administration decided to use the more limited authority. Unfortunately, using this authority for such an extended period, as discussed later, created nettlesome problems for the Army.

On January 18, 1991, two days after Operation Desert Storm commenced, the president finally invoked the broader authority contained in title 10, section 673. The administration had no intention of mobilizing 1 million reservists for two years, but the action enabled the Pentagon to exceed the 180-day maximum and to gain access to members of the Individual Ready Reserve, who had been exempted under the limited call-up authority. This was important, because many physicians and other reservists with critical skills were in the IRR.

The Pentagon authorized the services to call up to 360,000 reservists, but the war ended well before that number was reached. One-quarter million reservists had been mobilized by March 10, 1991, of which about 20,000 were members of the IRR (table 4-1).

By mid-January a sizable contingent of reserve combat forces had been deployed: four infantry battalions, two tank battalions, and an artillery

33. The Individual Ready Reserve is a pool of previously trained reservists who are not members of units and generally do not drill or get paid. For the most part, they are fulfilling enlistment obligations, but many are volunteers who desire to maintain a reserve affiliation.

34. Congressional Research Service, *Activation of Selected Reserves Under Executive Order 12727 and Executive Order 12733 For Service in the Arabian Peninsula*, report 90-563A (December 6, 1990).

regiment from the Marine Corps Reserve, and a tactical fighter wing, two tactical fighter groups, and a tactical reconnaissance group from the Air Force reserve components. Most reservists called up, however, were support personnel who provided services that, while vital to a military campaign, were less glamorous than combat activities and consequently received less news coverage.

More than 100,000 reservists served in the Persian Gulf area during Desert Shield and Desert Storm; the rest were either assigned to stateside positions or were still undergoing postmobilization training when the cease-fire went into effect. The Army accounted for 70 percent of deployed reservists, with 39,000 from the Army Reserve and 33,000 from the Army National Guard. The 62 reservists who lost their lives during the buildup and the military campaign accounted for 16 percent of all casualties, approximately their representation in the gulf (18 percent).[35]

All in all, the activation of reservists for the conflict appeared to proceed smoothly, especially when contrasted with previous mobilization experiences. Ironically, the most conspicuous issue, as in the Vietnam conflict, did not involve who *was* mobilized but who *was not*.

Roundout Brigades

The fact that most of the reserve units—and all the Army's units—in the initial call-up were support organizations caught the attention of many congressional supporters of the total force concept. They found the Pentagon's failure to mobilize the highly touted National Guard roundout brigades especially disconcerting.[36] According to all the pronouncements on the total force policy and by most understandings of the Pentagon's contingency plans, the 48th Mechanized Infantry Brigade (Georgia National Guard) and the 155th Armored Brigade (Mississippi National Guard) would be deployed with their parent active divisions—the 24th Mechanized Infantry and 1st Armored Cavalry, the first heavy divisions sent to the Arabian Peninsula. That they were not was embarrassing for legislators who had spearheaded efforts to revitalize the reserves. Some

35. Mark J. Eitelberg, "A Preliminary Assessment of Population Representation in Operations Desert Shield and Desert Storm," paper prepared for the 1991 Biennial Conference of the Inter-University Seminar on Armed Forces and Society, pp. 4–6, 31.

36. The two field artillery brigades that had been mobilized—the 142d from Arkansas and Oklahoma and the 196th from Tennessee, Kentucky, and West Virginia—are categorized as combat support by the Army.

were concerned that the substitution of active brigades for the roundout units would endanger future reserve funding.[37]

Representative Beverly Byron, chair of the Military Personnel and Compensation Subcommittee of the House Armed Services Committee, focused on an additional matter: "the nation has a right to know whether our investment in the reserves has been the right answer. . . . If it has not been the right answer, we need to change the course now before we build the force of the future."[38]

Funding and the organization of the military were valid concerns, especially in the case of the 48th Infantry Brigade, the centerpiece of the roundout concept. There were good reasons to expect that the 24th Division would have been deployed en toto, because the Army had ear-marked it for early deployment and had bestowed on its roundout brigade the highest equipment and training priorities.[39] The Pentagon noted, however, that the 24th was deployed before the decision to mobilize reservists and moreover, under the provisions of the call-up authority, the reserves would have been limited to 180 days of service, which was considered too short a period for them to be useful in Desert Shield. This argument was dismissed by critics, who said that the time limit could have been extended by a presidential declaration of a national emergency (which had already been made) or by legislation to change the provisions of the existing authority.

The issue erupted into a major controversy between the active Army and the national guard lobby that continued well beyond the end of the conflict. The debate focused on different understandings of the functions of roundout brigades and different assessments of their readiness.

MIXED SIGNALS. Since the establishment of the roundout concept, and especially since the brigades' status had been upgraded during the 1980s, a distinct—if unintended—impression had been left by both active and guard officials that the brigades, especially the 48th, could maintain a

37. The Army substituted the 197th Infantry Brigade for the 48th and the 1st Brigade of the 2d Armored Division for the 155th. The Pentagon's failure to call up the roundout brigades was criticized by Congressman Les Aspin, chairman of the House Armed Services Committee, who stated, "in Operation Desert Shield, the United States has a chance for a real test of the Total Force concept but we're not getting it." Memorandum from Les Aspin on the Pentagon, reserves, and Operation Desert Shield, October 16, 1990.

38. Rick Maze, "Reserves an Untapped Resource, Report Says," *Army Times*, October 29, 1990, p. 18.

39. There was less reason to expect that the 155th should have been deployed because its parent division was more closely associated with the European contingency and had been assigned a lower status in the Army priority system.

level of readiness that would permit them to deploy with their parent divisions. The commanding general of the 5th Infantry Division told the Senate Appropriations Committee in 1987, "I would take my roundout units to war tomorrow, if necessary." And General Norman Schwarzkopf, who had commanded the 24th Division from 1983 to 1985, had boasted, "Roundout is a fact of life . . . the 48th Brigade, Georgia Army National Guard, is the third brigade of my division. . . . I expect them to fight alongside us. They have demonstrated (their capability) through three demanding rotations at the National Training Center . . . they are, in fact, combat ready."[40]

Such optimistic statements by Army officials are often intended mainly to boost the morale of reservists and assuage their powerful champions on Capitol Hill. And although these statements were not taken literally by insiders, they nevertheless left a clear impression that the Guard brigades were essentially interchangeable with their active counterparts.

The Army National Guard obviously subscribed to this view. In fact, a former chief of the National Guard Bureau described the decision to provide the brigades with extensive postmobilization training as "the most blatant insult to the Guard in modern times." Pointing to seeming inconsistencies in the Pentagon's war plans, he stated,

> had the Soviets launched an attack on Western Europe, there would have been no consideration of further "workup"—the brigades would have been dispatched directly in accordance with the war plan to meet a far more capable enemy than Iraq. . . . Not many years ago the National Guard Bureau and . . . Department of the Army squared off on the stated views of at least one senior four-star Army commander that no Guard units should be deployed before six weeks of postmobilization training.
>
> To accept that would have disrupted every war plan that included early Guard participation and relegated the Guard to a later "follow-along" role. The Bureau prevailed. . . .[41]

But this view did not square with Army war plans, which reportedly assumed that "roundout brigades would not deploy with those active units which had to deploy within 10 days of mobilization . . . because of both requirements for post-mobilization training and an insufficiency of strategic sealift."[42]

---

40. Robert L. Goldich, *The Army's Roundout Concept after the Persian Gulf War* (Congressional Research Service, October 22, 1991), pp. 16, 17.

41. Herbert R. Temple, Jr., "Desert Shield: Retraining Is Not Needed," *National Guard* (February 1991), p. 17.

42. Goldich, *Army's Roundout Concept*, p. 18.

The clearest indication that the 48th Brigade might reasonably have been expected to be deployable immediately was the decision to select its parent 24th Division for Central Command, whose rapid-reaction mission would not appear to allow time for postmobilization training. But in a seeming contradiction, General Gordon R. Sullivan, chief of staff of the Army, discounted that connection, commenting in 1991 that "the round-outs originated to increase the strength of active divisions for major, protracted combat in Europe. They were not meant to be used as contingency forces for immediate, short duration deployments."[43]

Moreover, in testimony before Congress, based on the Persian Gulf experience, General Sullivan argued that more postmobilization training was needed to ready Guard units for combat. "We now know specifically what it takes to train people in combat brigades to fight," Sullivan testified. "In my opinion . . . we cannot train people to fight in combat brigades in less than ninety days [and] . . . we cannot train divisions to fight in less than 365 days."[44]

Summarizing the confusion of expectations about the deployability of the roundout brigades, Robert Goldich concluded,

> a variety of factors combined to create two fundamental misconceptions regarding the role of the roundout brigades in Army war plans prior to Desert Shield/Storm. First, many believed, or were led to believe by insufficient rigor in pre-Desert Shield war and mobilization planning, that roundout brigades could deploy without at least several weeks of postmobilization training. In fact, the issue appears to have received virtually no systematic and rigorous examination at high levels in either the active Army or the National Guard. Arguably, it took a war for such an examination to be forced on the Army.[45]

THE READINESS WRANGLE. Also at issue was whether the roundout brigades were ready for combat. How did their readiness compare with that of the active brigades? These questions, too, aroused heated debate between the Army's active and National Guard components and revealed major deficiencies in the Army's ability to gauge the readiness of a unit—active or reserve—for combat.

Pentagon officials and the active Army leadership were quick to retreat from the total force proclamations that had marked sixteen peacetime years. Now that a war might be in the offing, rhetoric gave way to reality.

43. Goldich, *Army's Roundout Concept*, pp. 17–18.
44. *Inside the Army*, March 2, 1992, p. 2.
45. Goldich, *Army's Roundout Concept*, p. 20.

When the three reserve combat brigades were finally mobilized, the Pentagon hedged on the decision concerning their subsequent deployment to Saudi Arabia until their training had been completed and their combat readiness had been assessed.

This announcement took many observers by surprise because they had presumed that such assessments were routinely made through monitoring systems established for that purpose. In fact, however, the system does not purport to measure combat readiness or capability, but rather resource and training status.[46] For example, a unit is considered to be in a C-1 status if it possesses the required resources and is trained to undertake the full wartime mission for which it is organized or designed. A unit equipped and trained to undertake the bulk of its wartime mission is rated C-2. One able to undertake major portions of the mission is considered C-3, and so forth.[47] These ratings also suggest how much time it will take a unit to attain a fully ready status. For battalions, brigades, and divisions, a C-2 rating indicates that the unit would require three to four weeks to get ready; a C-3 unit would require five to six weeks.[48]

Although it is understood that not all units can maintain C-1 status in peacetime, the Army chief of staff insisted that the guard combat brigades meet the standard before being deployed.[49] This conservative decision was consistent with the administration's commitment to minimize casualties. Secretary of Defense Cheney "made it clear from the beginning of Desert Shield that no military unit, Active or Reserve, would be

46. Before 1987 the services used the unit status and identity report (UNITREP) to categorize unit combat readiness. Units were assigned a rating, ranging from "fully combat ready" (C-1) to "not combat ready" (C-4), depending on the unit's percentage of wartime requirements for people and equipment and the estimated training time required to reach a fully trained status. A unit was also assigned an overall rating, usually the lowest of the category ratings, but subject to adjustment by unit commanders. Since these ratings "were erroneously viewed by some as a measure for unit readiness and/or capability when, in fact, the ratings only measured the status of a unit's resources and training," the Pentagon adopted the status of resources and training system (SORTS), an effort to downplay the combat readiness connotations. These changes, however, were largely cosmetic: combat condition ratings are now called category levels, equipment readiness is now called equipment condition, and descriptive short titles, such as "fully combat ready," have been omitted. *Reserve Component Programs, Fiscal Year 1987: Annual Report of the Reserve Forces Policy Board*, p. 160.

47. Goldich, *Army's Roundout Concept*, p. 35.

48. Congressional Budget Office, *Improving the Army Reserves* (November 1985), p. 17.

49. Les Aspin and William Dickinson, *Defense for a New Era: Lessons of the Persian Gulf War* (GPO, 1992), p. 59. The standard for combat support and combat service support units, however, was C-3 (p. 57).

sent into combat until it was ready. Any other policy would have been a disservice to the soldiers whose lives would have otherwise been at greater risk."[50]

When the roundout brigades were mobilized, one reported a C-2 level of readiness. Its commander predicted that the unit would require 28 days to become fully trained. The other two brigades reported a C-3 readiness level and anticipated 40 days of training to attain C-1 status. Based on their own assessments coincident with training plans used to prepare active brigades for the National Training Center (NTC), active Army officials called for 91 days of training for the 48th Brigade, 106 days for the 155th, and 135 days for the 256th—more than triple the original estimates and a clear indication that, at least from the active Army's standpoint, the peacetime ratings had been grossly inflated.[51]

These differing assessments ignited a controversy that pitted the Pentagon's leadership against the National Guard and its congressional supporters. The reserve lobby contended that the active Army's leadership was purposely underrating the roundout units. One of the most direct critics was Les Aspin, chairman of the House Armed Services Committee, who proclaimed, "I have heard a number of reasons for not sending Guard and Reserve combat units [to Saudi Arabia], but they are about as solid as sand. I suspect the most important factor is the active-force prejudice against using reserve forces."[52]

Guard officials were claiming, meanwhile, that Guard units were being held to a higher readiness standard than necessary, and certainly higher than their active counterparts. The readiness of the 48th Brigade, they claimed, was virtually identical to the two active Brigades in the 24th Division and, moreover, that the 197th Brigade that took the place of the 48th "had deployed to Saudi Arabia in C-5 status" because it had to convert from older M60 tanks to new M1s. The active Army was accused of changing the rules in midstream, and Guard officials bristled at the idea that they would have to meet higher standards for deployment at "the same time the commander of the active Army's 3d Armored Division (a first-line-of-defense unit in Europe) was saying . . . that despite two month's time in Saudi Arabia, his division still wasn't ready for

50. Department of Defense, "Conduct of the Persian Gulf Conflict," an interim report to the Congress (July 1991), p. 11-4.
51. General Accounting Office, *National Guard: Peacetime Training Did Not Adequately Prepare Combat Brigades for Gulf War* (September 1991), pp. 24, 25–26.
52. Quoted in Maze, "Reserves an Untapped Resource," p. 18.

combat."[53] An analysis done by the General Accounting Office at the request of Congressman G. V. (Sonny) Montgomery of Mississippi, however, found that by virtually any measure the active brigades were much more prepared than the Guard units they replaced.[54]

Primary attention was focused on the 48th Mechanized Infantry Brigade, considered the best of the roundout units. After spending a month at Fort Stewart, home of its parent 24th division, the 48th was sent to Fort Irwin in early January 1991, the largest combat formation ever to go through the National Training Center. Meanwhile the 155th and 256th Brigades were undergoing postmobilization training at Fort Hood, Texas.

The active Army committed considerable resources to train for the roundout brigades. By conservative estimate, 9,000 Army personnel were assigned to train the brigades at the individual, crew, and unit levels, a commitment that Army authorities felt had compromised the readiness of the 4th and 5th Infantry Divisions, two of the organizations responsible for the training.[55]

While the 48th was at NTC, its progress was followed by the media as closely as security permitted. The dismissal of its brigade commander and the extension of its training period by several weeks was widely reported. Army spokesmen contended that the unit "suffered from deficient leadership and training, poorly maintained equipment and key personnel sidelined with medical conditions."[56] Army trainers identified "severe weaknesses in the basic leadership skills of NCO's in each of the three brigades," including "a lack of initiative, of discipline, of proficiency in basic soldiering skills, and a 'so what' attitude." Guard officers, too, were criticized for technical and tactical incompetence, an inability to set standards, and problems with enforcing discipline.[57]

Leadership problems were also highlighted in an internal report prepared by the Army's inspector general: "Of the several weaknesses noted in the brigades, poor leadership especially in NCO ranks . . . and field grade officers, appeared the most debilitating. Lacking technical and tactical skills, many leaders could not make routine operations happen

53. Unpublished letter from Major General Robert F. Ensslin, Jr., president of the National Guard Association of the United States, to the editor of the *Brookings Review*, July 15, 1991.

54. General Accounting Office, *Army Training: Replacement Brigades Were More Proficient Than Guard Roundout Brigades* (November 1992), p. 2.

55. General Accounting Office, *National Guard*, p. 27.

56. "The Little Unit That Couldn't," *Time*, June 10, 1991, p. 19.

57. General Accounting Office, *National Guard*, pp. 17–18.

routinely. They demonstrated poor knowledge, insight, and command and control of daily activities."[58] Some members of the 48th were equally critical of their unit's leadership, with one guardsman indicating that while "we performed pretty well at the company levels, at battalion and brigade levels, it didn't go too well. There was not enough cohesion."[59]

National Guard officials saw the situation differently. According to the chief of the National Guard Bureau, "the brigade completed training with exceptional success. . . . The soldiers were dedicated and enthusiastic."[60] Perhaps the harshest criticism of the regular Army came from Major General Robert F. Ensslin, Jr., president of the National Guard Association, who concluded that "Round-out did not fail. The (active) army failed to implement and follow its own policies." According to press accounts, Ensslin also contended that

> the Army had labeled the Georgia 48th Infantry Brigade unready for combat even though it set records at the National Training Center. The Army had changed the rules in the middle, forcing new equipment on Guard units at the last minute . . . . The Army had just plain cheated, manipulating readiness standards to send less-ready regular units to Saudi Arabia, even though they scored lower than the Guard's round-out brigades.[61]

Conflicting views were even reported among active Army officers responsible for conducting training at the National Training Center. The commander of the NTC's elite OPFOR (opposing forces) unit concluded that the 48th was "as good as some of the finest brigades, and at platoon and company level, better than most."[62] However, according to Colonel James Hedgepeth, NTC operations officer, "we don't rate or compare anybody. There are no scores, no numbers. . . . If the Georgia guys want bragging rights, they can't find them here."[63] The 48th was finally certified combat ready on February 28, fifty-one days after it began training

58. *Special Assessment: National Guard Brigades' Mobilization* (Department of the Army Inspector General, June 1991), p. 3-7.

59. Gary Hendricks, "The 48th Georgia Guardsmen Blame Unit's Unreadiness on Officers," *Atlanta Journal–The Atlanta Constitution*, March 6, 1991, p. A7.

60. Statement of Lieutenant General John B. Conaway, Chief, National Guard Bureau, in *The Impact of the Persian Gulf War and the Decline of the Soviet Union on How the United States Does Its Defense Business*, Hearings before the House Committee on Armed Services, 102 Cong. 1 sess. (GPO, 1991), p. 183.

61. Quoted in Robert Unger, "Army Guard Digs in for Battle as Cuts in Federal Budget Loom," *Kansas City Star*, September 23, 1991, p. 1.

62. Attributed to Colonel Patrick O'Neal in a letter to the editor, *Armed Forces Journal International*, by Chris Nichols, Georgia National Guard, May 1991, p. 6.

63. Unger, "Army Guard Digs In."

and perhaps coincidentally on the day that the ground war was suspended and the cease-fire announced by President Bush. The unit returned to Georgia during the week of March 4 and was deactivated.

The training and validation of the other two roundout brigades was interrupted by the end of the conflict. The 155th had been scheduled to be validated as combat ready on March 22, 1991, and the 256th on April 13.[64] The longer periods of time between mobilization and validation, 105 and 135 days, respectively, for these units were attributed to a lack of training facilities and personnel and, in the case of the 256th, the need to become qualified in a new weapon system—the Bradley fighting vehicle.[65]

Reserve combat brigade readiness and deployability continued to attract wide attention following the conflict and became the subject of various investigations and analyses. The Army's inspector general and the National Guard Bureau issued separate reports in June 1991 reflecting vastly different interpretations of the events surrounding the failure to deploy, including the readiness of the units and the validity of training standards.

In September the General Accounting Office issued an assessment that found substantial confusion and misunderstanding surrounding the deployment of roundout units and passed the blame around.

> The Army has not adequately prepared its National Guard roundout brigades to be fully ready to deploy quickly. When the three brigades were activated, many soldiers were not completely trained to do their jobs; many noncommissioned officers were not adequately trained in leadership skills; and Guard members had difficulty adjusting to the active Army's administrative systems for supply and personnel management. . . . Also, when activated, many soldiers had serious medical or dental conditions that would have delayed or prevented their deployment.
>
> The activation of the three roundout brigades also revealed that the post-mobilization training plans prepared by the three brigades during peacetime had underestimated the training that would be necessary for them to be fully combat ready. The plans were based on peacetime evaluation reports that Army officials believed overstated the brigade's proficiency and training readiness. After the brigades were activated, active

64. Goldich, *Army's Roundout Concept*, p. 14.

65. Goldich, *Army's Roundout Concept*, p. 14. The 256th Infantry Brigade attracted wide media attention during its training period at Fort Hood, Texas, when sixty-seven guardsmen, protesting poor treatment, returned to Shreveport, Louisiana, and were declared absent without leave. Gary Hendricks, "31 Soldiers Punished for AWOL," *Atlanta Constitution*, February 27, 1991, p. 7.

Army trainers developed substantially revised training plans calling for over three times the number of training days estimated in readiness reports and requiring the support of almost 9,000 active Army trainers and other personnel.[66]

In the final analysis the evidence strongly indicates that both the active Army and the Army National Guard had overestimated the capabilities of the Guard combat brigades, a misjudgment that could have had important consequences had the conflict been more protracted.

Mobilization of Support Forces

Although the delay in mobilizing and the failure to deploy the National Guard roundout brigades dominated much of the news coverage of the reserve's participation in the Persian Gulf conflict, many Army reservists and guardsmen were deployed to the Arabian peninsula in various combat support activities, such as artillery units, and combat service support functions, such as supply and transportation, military police, medical, and water purification units.

The largest and most rapid deployment of U.S. military forces since World War II was deemed a success, and reserve participation was widely heralded. A postwar review of the mobilization by the General Accounting Office, however, revealed important problems that, had the Army not enjoyed the luxury of a six-month buildup and had the war not been terminated so quickly, could have seriously compromised the campaign. Brought into question were restrictions imposed by the extended use of limited mobilization authority, inefficiencies created by the incremental call-up of reservists, and difficulties in assessing unit readiness.

CALL-UP AUTHORITY. It was no surprise that the administration chose initially to mobilize reservists under the limited authority of title 10, section 673b. The situation was not only tailor made for these provisions, but Congress had been chiding the administration for its failure to use the option. As the buildup proceeded, however, the limitations of the authority "introduced inefficiencies into the force selection process; prevented access to some needed reserves; and, in some cases, led the Army to exclude trained reservists from the operation due to their initial unavailability."[67]

---

66. General Accounting Office, *National Guard*, p. 3.
67. General Accounting Office, *Operation Desert Storm*, p. 15.

The inability to call up members of the Individual Ready Reserve, for example, hampered readying mobilized support units. Under total force contingency planning, the Army had assumed that the limited authority that precluded mobilizing the IRR would be an *initial* step, followed quickly by the less restrictive provisions of partial mobilization authority. Thus it had planned on the early availability of IRR personnel to bring both active and reserve support units up to wartime standards and to fill vacancies created by members unable to meet deployment criteria. Instead, the Army had to rely on reserve volunteers, retirees, and people transferred from other units.[68]

Further, because reservists called up under the limited authority could serve for only 90 days (extendable to 180 days), the Army delayed mobilizing some units to hedge against the possibility that replacement units would be needed within three to six months. This rationing taxed the Army's capabilities, especially those (such as water purification units) that were already in short supply.

INCREMENTALISM AND ITS CONSEQUENCES. Given the uncertainties stemming from events unfolding in the Persian Gulf, the administration's cautious approach to mobilizing reserves was understandable. The initial call-up in August was limited to less than 50,000 personnel total and 25,000 for the Army, ceilings that were raised to 125,000 and 80,000, respectively, in November, to 188,000 and 115,000 in December, and finally, under the expanded partial mobilization authority, to 360,000 and 220,000 in January. This piecemeal buildup, however, limited the flexibility of Army officials to provide ready support units. Faced on one hand with the ceiling on reserve call-ups and the stipulation that reservists could only be called up as units and on the other with the requirement to provide the support capabilities specified by the theater commander the Army created subunits within larger reserve units so that it could call up only essential portions of a unit. This scheme, according to the GAO, "(1) adversely affected the deploying unit's integrity and morale, (2) adversely affected the ability of the partial unit left behind to deploy, and (3) created a time-consuming administrative bureaucracy."[69]

The mobilization ceilings also prompted the Army to substitute active personnel for reservists in command and control units that had been

68. General Accounting Office, *Operation Desert Storm*, p. 17.

69. It has been estimated that the 25,000 ceiling in the initial call-up fell some 55,000 short of the Army's calculated requirement for support personnel. General Accounting Office, *Operation Desert Storm*, p. 23.

expected to be mobilized and deployed. Because these units are staffed with senior officers, many reservists were skeptical of the rationale, especially since the Army had a history of replacing senior reserve officers in previous mobilizations.[70] "Not affording the reserves the opportunity to perform the demanding roles they have been assigned and for which they have been trained" was considered by the GAO an inefficient use of resources and damaging to the morale of the reserve forces.[71]

WERE THE SUPPORT UNITS READY? In contrast with the C-1 readiness status required for combat brigades, the Army had established a liberal C-3 standard as the level necessary for combat support and combat service support units. This meant that a unit could deploy with as few as 70 percent of its personnel, as little as 65 percent of its on-hand equipment and 60 percent of its high-priority equipment deemed mission capable, and could require five to six weeks to attain a fully capable C-1 status.[72]

Army officials were hampered in their efforts to identify the readiness of the support units because of weaknesses in status reports. Lack of uniformity in report guidelines and wide discretion enjoyed by local commanders in reporting shortages, for example, put a heavier burden on officials charged with validating readiness. Between August and early November 1990, 15 percent of Army reserve component units reporting to their mobilization stations were unable to meet the C-3 criteria. The situation deteriorated as less ready units were mobilized; between November 1990 and mid-January 1991, for example, 34 percent of the units were not deployable. "By the end of the mobilization," a congressional investigation concluded, "Forces Command had nearly exhausted its ability to put together the kind of support units needed in Southwest Asia."[73]

70. The most extensive substitution took place during the mobilization for World War II when the Army substituted regulars for virtually all National Guard officers above the rank of lieutenant colonel and for an extremely high percentage of those in the lower officer ranks. I. Heymont and E. W. McGregor, *Review and Analysis of Recent Mobilizations and Deployments of US Army Reserve Components* (McLean, Va: Research and Analysis Corp., October 1972), p. 2-8.

71. General Accounting Office, *Operation Desert Storm*, p. 25.

72. Binkin and Kaufmann, *U.S. Army Guard and Reserve*, p. 92. Even then, the Army found it increasingly difficult to provide support units that met this standard, because the pool of critical units was becoming exhausted. "By the end of the mobilization period," it was reported, "the Army had called up eight of the nine guard medium truck companies, eight of the nine guard evacuation hospitals, all six guard water purification units and 71 of the 119 military police units." Les Aspin and William Dickinson, *Defense for a New Era: Lessons of the Persian Gulf War* (GPO, 1992), p. 57.

73. Aspin and Dickinson, *Defense for a New Era*, pp. 57–58. As one example of the

In its official assessment of the Gulf conflict, however, the Pentagon accentuated the positive, concluding that "most units of the Reserve components were ready to be deployed on schedule and the timing and sequence of their deployment was determined by the needs of the theater and similar factors, rather than by postmobilization training requirements."[74]

MISSION PERFORMANCE. In the final analysis, the effectiveness of military units lies in how well they perform the mission for which they were designed. Measuring performance is often difficult. Performance in some missions, such as a tactical fighter campaign in which the targets destroyed provide a reasonable gauge of effectiveness, is easier to measure than performance where results are less well defined, as with a military police unit, a civil affairs unit, or many other support activities.

Nonetheless, as would be expected in the wake of such an overwhelming victory, praise for the performance of reservists was universal. President Bush declared in an address before Congress on March 6, 1991 that "this victory belongs . . . to the regulars, to the reserves, to the National Guard." Secretary Cheney noted that "we could not have done what we did in the Gulf without the tremendous performance of a quarter of a million Reservists. . . . They did everything, and they did it extremely well."[75] One of the strongest endorsements of the reserves' performance was provided at a conference of the Reserve Officers Association by the commander of the logistics operation during Desert Storm, who indicated that the massive movement of ground forces would not have been possible without reservists. Especially impressed with members of the Individual Ready Reserve, the general said that "It totally amazed me how well you trained these people."[76] Based on these assessments, and lacking detailed data for comparing active and reserve unit performance, one can only assume that all units accomplished their missions with equal proficiency.

---

kinds of problems that arose during mobilization, in some of the California National Guard units, 80 percent of the members "were unable to meet active-duty physical fitness standards," according to Brigadier General Daniel Brennan. In some units, only two of every ten reservists were able initially to pass the test, but eventually all twelve units called to active duty during the crisis met deployment criteria. See Steve Gibson, "Guards Flunked Fitness," *Sacramento Bee*, June 18, 1991, p. B1.

74. Department of Defense, *Conduct of the Persian Gulf War* (April 1992), p. 480.

75. Quoted in statement of Stephen M. Duncan in *Department of Defense Authorization for Appropriations for Fiscal Years 1992 and 1993*, Hearings, pt. 6, p. 443.

76. Comments of Lieutenant General William Pagonis in Greg Seigle, "Desert Storm Support Draws Rave Reviews," *Army Times*, February 3, 1992, p. 10.

Implications for Force Planning

The Desert Shield mobilization was a valuable, though limited, test of the total force policy, in some cases confirming and in others dispelling critics' concerns. First, President Bush's quick decision to call up the reserves laid to rest the fears, born during the Vietnam era, that the potential political cost would deter the nation's chief executive from ordering mobilization. Second, notwithstanding some administrative and procedural problems, the mobilization and deployment of reserve units was successful, especially when measured against previous experience. But there is no publicly available analysis that has assessed the performance of the units—active or reserve—with any degree of scientific rigor.

The controversy surrounding the combat roundout brigades brought the total force concept under closer scrutiny, but whether the failure to deploy these brigades should be attributed to a lack of combat readiness or to bureaucratic rivalries remains unclear. In any event, although this experience might not have diminished the value of the policy, it seriously weakened the case for assigning to reserve units missions that would require their early deployment.

Meanwhile, this first wartime test of the total force, which had been expected to help the Pentagon's Total Force Policy Study Group address many matters of concern, instead made it more difficult for the group to meet its deadlines. Some of the problems were reflected in its interim report, submitted to Congress in September 1990, which was long on description, short on analysis, contained few recommendations, and was especially vague about future roles for the reserve forces.[77] Understandably, the group was buying time, hoping that some of the uncertainties would be dispelled by the Gulf experience.

The interim report stirred controversy within the reserves because it differed substantially from a favorable initial draft that had proposed reserve units be used for short-term mobilizations, including early-deploying combat missions. The proposal had run counter to a new force structure being developed at the Pentagon, which envisioned a less prominent role for reserve forces in the post–cold war world. "The [interim] report should make clear," wrote the Pentagon's under secretary for policy, "that we expect this strategy to lead to both active and reserve force structure reductions, and begin to build a case for this position. The draft's suggestions of moving additional forces into reserves and its

77. Department of Defense, *Total Force Policy Interim Report.*

leaning toward expanded reserve roles do the opposite." The under secretary also criticized the study group's subsequent revisions: "the paper still exhibits the general reserve-favorable tilt of the previous draft."[78]

In a sense, these differences between the Total Force Policy Study Group and the Pentagon's planners were understandable in light of the scope and pace of changes taking place in national security policy but they also strongly hinted of a coming struggle between the military services and their civilian masters over the evolving force structure.

The suggestion that the study group was being urged, regardless of analytical justification, to support a predetermined force structure was discomforting, especially to supporters of reserve forces. But as expected, the defense secretary's staff prevailed and the final report of the study group in December 1990 was essentially a tract supporting the base force, so called because it represented "a capability below which forces may no longer be adequate to underwrite vital strategic objectives."[79]

The base force plan, to be described in more detail later, provided a basis for the administration's fiscal year 1992 defense budget and fiscal year 1993–97 defense program. The Pentagon proposed cutting the active forces by 17 percent (from 2.0 million to 1.63 million) between 1991 and 1995 (table 4-2). The reserves also would be reduced by 19 percent, from 1.14 million to 0.9 million. As a first installment of that program, the Pentagon proposed to cut 106,000 people from the active-duty rolls in fiscal year 1992 and about the same number of reservists.

The proposed cuts in active personnel were readily endorsed by the congressional armed services committees, but the planned reductions in the reserves were rejected by both. The House committee was willing to cut 37,580 reservists; the Senate committee would allow a reduction of only 32,700.[80] In conference, the House committee position prevailed, authorizing a Selected Reserve strength of 1,151,046 for fiscal year 1992. The committee also expected that "any changes proposed by the Department of Defense to Selected Reserve strengths and associated force

78. Rick Maze, "Reserve Study Called 'Political Brochure,'" *Army Times*, June 17, 1991, p. 6.

79. Comments of Lieutenant General George L. Butler, cited in "Base Force Idea is 'Tailored to New and Enduring Strategic Reality,'" *Aerospace Daily*, October 9, 1990, p. 39.

80. *National Defense Authorization Act for Fiscal Years 1992 and 1993*, H. Rept. 102-60, 102 Cong. 1 sess. (GPO, 1991), p. 235; and *National Defense Authorization Act for Fiscal Years 1992 and 1993*, S. Rept. 102-113, 102 Cong. 1 sess. (GPO, 1991), p. 201.

Table 4-2. *Military Personnel Levels Proposed under the Base Force Plan, Fiscal Years 1991 and 1997, by Service and Component, as of January 1992*

Thousands

Service and component	1991	1997	Percent change
Active			
Army	725	536	−26
Navy	571	501	−12
Marine Corps	195	159	−18
Air Force	511	430	−16
Total Active	2,002	1,626	−19
Selected Reserve			
Army National Guard	441	338	−23
Army Reserve	300	229	−24
Navy Reserve	151	118	−22
Marine Corps Reserve	44	35	−20
Air National Guard	118	118	0
Air Force Reserve	84	82	−3
Total Selected Reserve	1,138	920	−19

Sources: Active strengths from Keith Berner and Stephen Daggett, *Defense Budget for FY 1993: Data Summary* (Congressional Research Service, February 10, 1992). Reserve strengths from William Matthews, "How Much Is Enough?" *Navy Times*, April 6, 1992, p. 11.

structure levels in fiscal year 1994 and beyond will be made on the basis of an analytically supported rationale."[81]

Thus, as it had so often in the past, Congress again came to the reserves' rescue, compelled not only by the lobbying by the National Guard Association and the Reserve Officers Association but by its suspicion that the Pentagon's decision to reduce the military's reliance on reserves was based more on parochialism than on rigorous analysis. Key members of Congress were leery of the total force study to begin with, unable to fathom why the Pentagon would advocate a lesser role for the reserves in the face of their reported performance in the Persian Gulf and the fact that they represent such a bargain in national security. Senator John Glenn, for example, criticized the Pentagon's recommendations as "simplistic, potentially damaging to the combat readiness of our military services and potentially damaging to our communities." Glenn went on to say he would be "willing to make reductions in the Guard and Reserve that are justified by analysis. If cuts from such anal-

81. *National Defense Authorization Act for Fiscal Years 1992 and 1993*, conference report 102-311, 102 Cong. 1 sess. (GPO, 1991), p. 537.

ysis fall in my state, and they make sense, I would support them. Together, the Defense Department and Congress must work to achieve the
most combat-capable force the nation can devise—regular and reserve—
which I am sure is a goal we all share."[82]

Accordingly, the Defense Authorization Act mandated "a study . . .
that is independent of the military departments" to examine active and
reserve structures and mixes and that "comprehensive analytic information" be provided to the Pentagon that would evaluate the "mix or mixes
of reserve and active forces . . . that are considered acceptable to carry
out expected future military missions."[83] The act further specified that
the study consider what was obviously Congress's preferred option: "an
FY 1997 force with the same selected-reserve end strength it authorized
for fiscal year 1993. . . . This force should cost the same as the projected
DoD Base Force, but would use 215,796 more selected reserve personnel
than does the DoD base force."[84]

The controversy was renewed in January 1992 when the Pentagon
submitted its fiscal 1993 budget and fiscal 1992–97 six-year defense plan
to Congress. The administration continued to plan for an eighteen-divi-
sion Army of twelve active and six national guard divisions, plus two
cadre divisions, and proposed that the Selected Reserves be reduced by
116,000 in fiscal 1993 and 198,000 by fiscal 1995. The Army reserve
components would bear the brunt of these reductions, dropping by 92,000
in 1993 and 166,000 by 1995.[85]

In March 1992, in response to requests by Congress for more specifics,
the Pentagon released a detailed plan for reducing the reserve components. It included a list of 830 reserve units to be reduced or inactivated

82. John Glenn, "Meat Ax Doesn't Cut It in Reserve Force Reduction," *Army Times*,
August 24, 1992, p. 25.

83. *National Defense Authorization Act for Fiscal Years 1992 and 1993*, conference report
102-311, pp. 62–63.

84. National Defense Research Institute, *Assessing the Structure and Mix of Future
Active and Reserve Forces: Interim Report to the Secretary of Defense* (Santa Monica, Calif.:
RAND, 1992), p. 21.

85. Office of the Assistant Secretary of Defense for Public Affairs, "DOD To Slow Pace
of Modernization, Cut Strategic Nuclear Arsenal While Maintaining Essential Forces,"
news release 26-92, January 29, 1992. A cadre is a skeleton organization composed of key
officer and enlisted personnel who can form, administer, and train a new unit. Widely used
by other nations (Israel and Switzerland, for example), cadres have not been extensively
employed by the United States since World War II. The Army's original plan to keep cadre
divisions at 20 percent of their wartime strength was later revised to provide for a strength
level of 70 percent, or 11,500 troops per division.

in fiscal years 1992–93, 80 percent of which had been intended to support active duty units assigned to the defense of Europe, which were also being eliminated. The remaining units, according to the secretary were "no longer needed in light of other changes in the world security picture and reduced defense budgets." The Pentagon was quick to point out that even following these reductions, there would still be 16 percent more reserve personnel at the end of fiscal 1993 than in fiscal 1980. The level of active personnel would be 13 percent lower.[86]

The proposal encountered the expected resistance in Congress, which was being "inundated with letters from guardsmen trying to save their units from the ax."[87] Their efforts did not go unrewarded. The House Armed Services Committee restored nearly 37,000 of the proposed 48,000 cuts in the Army National Guard, keeping it at 420,000, but only 5,500 of the 44,000 cuts proposed for the Army Reserve, allowing it to drop to 263,000. The House Appropriations Committee subsequently restored an additional 10,000 spaces for the Army Reserve.[88] The Senate Armed Services Committee, meanwhile, settled on 425,450 for the Army Guard and 296,230 for the Army Reserve. The final conference figures were 422,725 and 279,615, which was 40,000 more than the administration's request for the Guard and about 20,000 more for the Reserve.[89]

The conferees also adopted a House Armed Services Committee initiative for the Army National Guard "designed to pave the way for an expanded role for combat units in the future." The initiative called for increasing the experience and improving leadership training in the National Guard, concentrating on individual and small unit training, "leaving longer unit training for the period after mobilization," and establishing stricter medical, dental, and physical screening. It also proposed devising compatible Armywide personnel, maintenance, supply, and financial systems and improving the readiness reporting system and requiring active units to have a larger role in assessing their associated Guard units. Finally, the initiative directed the Army "to integrate the

86. Office of the Assistant Secretary of Defense for Public Affairs, "DOD Specifies Guard and Reserve Units to Eliminate," news release 114-92, March 26, 1992.

87. William Matthews, " 'Pushy' Million Mobilized," *Army Times*, April 20, 1992, p. 14. Congressional staff described the lobbying guardsmen as "very vocal," "very pushy," "very myopic," and "not very open to suggestion."

88. Grant Willis, "Panel Stays Firm on Reserves," *Army Times*, August 3, 1992, p. 20.

89. House Armed Services Committee, "Bill Promotes Military and Economic Security," news release, October 1, 1992, appendix table.

Guards in its planning for regional contingencies, and allocate resources accordingly."[90]

Where Do the Reserves Go from Here?

As my analysis has indicated, the size and composition of the nation's reserve forces depend on an array of military, economic, bureaucratic, and political factors, each of which has been affected in some way by the end of the cold war and the lessons of the Persian Gulf conflict. These factors need to be taken into account in the design of future reserve forces.

The Changing Military Rationale for the Reserves

An appropriate balance of active and reserve forces should rest principally on an assessment of military requirements—the forces considered necessary to meet the objectives of national security strategy. Such an assessment depends on many technical assumptions, including the size and nature of the threats to U.S. national security, the simultaneity of those threats, and the amount of warning before the start of hostilities. How that force should then be allocated among active and reserve components in turn depends on the readiness of those components to deploy and, once deployed, on their abilities to perform their assigned missions.

READINESS CONSIDERATIONS. In their opposing views of an appropriate mix of active and reserve forces, the administration and Congress are ignoring the valuable, if limited, experience gained from the Persian Gulf conflict. In designing the base force with a greatly diminished dependence on the reserves, Pentagon planners disregarded the evidence from the conflict that reserve support units can be mobilized early and used effectively. And in limiting the Pentagon's reduction of reserve forces, Congress ignored the evidence that combat units in the Army's reserve forces showed a serious lack of readiness that could be extremely difficult to rectify.

Differences in the readiness of combat and support units should not have taken anyone by surprise; they are inherent in the nature of their missions and the training required to attain appropriate skills. As a rule,

90. House Armed Services Committee, "Bill Promotes Military," pp. 18–20.

the readiness of support units depends on the proficiency of its individual members. The performance of combat formations, however, depends not only on the skills of members but on their ability to function as a team, with a premium on coordination, cohesion, and group chemistry. As ground warfare has become more complicated, in fact, attaining proficiency has become a more daunting task for part-time units, as explained by the commander of the Army Forces Command.

> For the Reserve Component, achieving readiness to operate successfully on the dynamic battlefield evidenced in Operation DESERT STORM requires intensive training after mobilization. . . . Roundout infantry and armor units must become expert at synchronizing complex battlefield systems such as Army aviation, air defense, direct and indirect fire support, command and control, intelligence, engineer, close air support and logistics to fight and survive on the battlefield. Proficiency with these synchronization tasks comes with rigorous, repetitive collective training at company level and above. It should not be surprising that combat maneuver roundout units require significantly more postmobilization training than combat support and combat service support units. The complex and unforgiving nature of these tasks and difficulty in training them during weekend drill periods pose a difficult challenge.[91]

From these conclusions, and supported by the roundout brigade controversy, the Army urged its National Guard component to plan for combat unit training at lower than brigade level. According to General Gordon Sullivan, the Army chief of staff, "normal Guard [combat unit] training periods should concentrate on the basics. . . . Tank crews and platoons must be proficient because they are building blocks for larger parent unit operations. When that is accomplished, and as resources permit, higher-level collective training can be conducted."[92] The Army thus has come full circle; company-level readiness had been the training objective for National Guard units when the total force concept was first

91. Statement of General Edwin H. Burba, Jr., commander in chief, Forces Command, in *Impact of Persian Gulf War*, Hearings, pp. 169–70.

92. Tom Donnelly, "Sullivan Putting New Spin on Roundout Brigades," *Army Times*, September 16, 1991, p. 10. The Army formalized the concept with the implementation of pilot programs designed to improve the quality of training and increase the readiness of its National Guard and Reserve combat units. Bold Shift is a revamped training program designed for reserve units that are affiliated with active units. The reserve training concept serves a similar purpose for unaffiliated reserve combat units. Both are expected to overcome the lack of training and readiness encountered during the Persian Gulf mobilization. For descriptions of these programs, see Greg Seigle, "Back to Basics," *Army Times*, September 7, 1992, p. 13; and Ron Martz, "Shaping Up Guard, Reserves," *Atlanta Constitution*, August 17, 1992, p. 3.

conceived, with battalion, brigade, and division staff training to be conducted following mobilization.[93]

At the extreme, some have argued that given their inherent training problems the Army's reserve components should not be assigned a combat mission at all. One such recommendation came from an unlikely source, the Army National Guard adviser to the U.S. Army War College.

> The Active Component (AC) is best suited to conduct combat operations, particularly the contingency type we may expect in the future; the Reserve Components (RC) are best at providing combat support and combat service support. Support missions offer distinct recruiting advantages, depend less on accessibility to large training areas, and are most compatible with executing the peacetime mission role of the Army.[94]

There have been no serious proposals, however, to strip the National Guard of its highly prized combat role; but a future shift in emphasis deserves consideration.

FORCE STRUCTURE CONSIDERATIONS. Strictly from national security considerations, the size and character of the reserve components in the past four decades have been dictated by the prospect of a conflict in central Europe involving NATO and the Warsaw Pact. This link became most evident in the early 1970s with the end of conscription and the adoption of the total force concept. Reliance on the reserves, especially by the Army and Air Force, grew to an unprecedented extent as planners envisaged requirements that far exceeded the capabilities that could be provided by the active forces alone. In the mid-1980s, for example, of a total of thirty-three division-size combat formations available to meet simultaneous threats of a major war in Europe accompanied by a smaller conflict elsewhere, eleven were reserve components. Roughly the same proportion of tactical fighter wings (thirteen of forty) were in the Air Force and Marine reserves. In addition, a large part of the support infrastructure, especially for the Army's deployed forces, was in the reserves. It was anticipated that many reserve units would be ready to deploy very early in a conflict, some with their parent active units, and most needing only minimal postmobilization training.

By 1990, with the collapse of communism, the disintegration of the Warsaw Pact, and the fragmentation of the Soviet military machine, the

93. Martin Binkin, *U.S. Reserve Forces: The Problem of the Weekend Warrior* (Brookings, 1974), p. 10.

94. Philip A. Brehm, *Restructuring the Army: The Road to a Total Force* (Strategic Studies Institute, U.S. Army War College, 1992), p. 1. Colonel Brehm, it should be noted, is a Signal Corps officer.

threat of a war in central Europe had diminished dramatically, and the idea of fighting one major and one minor war simultaneously became obsolete. Military strategists and force planners faced problems of identifying the remaining threats to U.S. security and devising new force planning assumptions.

The search for a new strategic concept was no mean task. Even Colin Powell, chairman of the Joint Chiefs, professed difficulty in identifying military threats: "Think hard about it," he said. "I'm running out of demons. I'm running out of villains. I'm down to Castro and Kim Il Sung."[95]

In early 1991, in the base force plan, its first comprehensive articulation of a post–cold war strategic concept, the Pentagon warned of the dangers still posed by the uncertain future of the Soviet Union, pointing out that "the Soviet military will remain, by a wide margin, the largest armed force on the [European] continent" and that "local sources of instability and oppression will continue to foster conflicts small and large in areas of interest to the United States."[96] The Pentagon unveiled a new conventional defense strategy, the main elements of which were forward military presence in regions crucial to U.S. security interests; the ability to respond to crises that might erupt; and the ability to reconstitute military capabilities to hedge against the reemergence of a superpower threat.

Five possible contingencies that could require the intervention of U.S. conventional military forces were identified: an insurgency or narcotics activity; a lesser regional contingency, unidentified by country or location; two major regional contingencies, one in Korea and another in Southwest Asia; and a war in Europe, perhaps escalating from a crisis involving a renewed Soviet threat.[97]

Additional texture was provided in a planning document leaked to the news media in early 1992. The "1994–99 Defense Planning Guidance Scenario Set" identified seven hypothetical situations that could lead to U.S. military involvement. These were to provide the basis upon which the services were to plan their forces and budgets:

1. NATO responds to an invasion of Lithuania by military forces of the republics of Russia and Belarus. About twelve U.S. Army divisions are

95. Jim Wolffe, "Powell Outlines Plan for Small, Versatile Force of the Future," *Air Force Times*, April 15, 1991, p. 3.

96. Department of Defense, *1991 Joint Military Net Assessment* (March 1991), p. ii.

97. Department of Defense, *1991 Joint Military Net Assessment*, p. 9-2.

involved and NATO forces prevail in 89 days of combat, including a three-week "very high intensity" counterattack.

2. A reprise of the Persian Gulf conflict occurs when Iraq, following a period of rearmament, again invades Kuwait, but this time continues into Saudi Arabia. A coalition is again formed, with close to five U.S. Army divisions and a Marine expeditionary force committed. The U.S.-led coalition wins in 54 days, including a seven-day "very high intensity" counterattack.

3. A surprise attack launched by North Korea aimed at reunification by force is met by a military force led by South Korea, including a U.S. contribution of more than five Army divisions and two Marine expeditionary forces. An allied victory is envisaged after 91 days of combat, including 28 days of "very high intensity" conflict.

4. A coup in Panama that threatens to close the Canal and put 15,000 American and other foreign nationals at risk is countered by employing simultaneously airborne and amphibious operations involving two airborne brigades, two Ranger battalions, and a Marine amphibious brigade. The U.S. wins in eight days of mid-intensity combat.

5. Three hundred American workers at Subic Bay Naval Base are taken hostage following a coup in the Philippines. The United States military forces, mounting three simultaneous landings with a Ranger regiment, an airborne infantry brigade, an amphibious brigade, and a brigade or more of light infantry, prevails in seven days of mid-intensity conflict.

6. With simultaneous attacks by Iraq and North Korea, the U.S. fights one war at a time, responding first in the Persian Gulf, before turning attention to Korea. In this case, the Iraqi forces are vanquished by a U.S.-led coalition in 70 days and the defeat of North Korea requires an additional 157 days.

7. In the worst case scenario, a "resurgent/emergent global threat"—presumably Russia or perhaps Japan—develops beginning in 1994 and, by 2001, is ready to begin a second cold war period or to launch a major global war. The United States "reconstitutes" its depleted military forces, but only after years of political debate. No time period is specified for this scenario.[98]

To meet these potential threats, the Pentagon envisioned a conventional force structure organized into three packages: contingency forces, Atlantic forces, and Pacific forces, with three associated organizational commands.

The contingency command, a new title for the rapid deployment force, would respond to often unpredictable crises in the third world. Its

98. Barton Gellman, "Pentagon War Scenario Spotlights Russia," *Washington Post*, February 20, 1992, p. 1. The Pentagon subsequently discarded the Lithuania contingency, according to one source, "because of publicity and poor taste." William W. Kaufmann, *Assessing the Base Force: How Much Is Too Much?* (Brookings, 1992), p. 48.

Table 4-3. *Allocation of Forces, Base Force Plan, 1995*

Force	Atlantic command	Pacific command	Contingency command	Total
Army (divisions)				
Active	5	2	5	12
Reserve	6	. . .	. . .	6
Cadre	2	. . .	. . .	2
Marine Corps (divisions/wings)				
Active	1/1	1/1	1/1	3/3
Reserve	1	. . .	. . .	1
Air Force (wings)				
Active	5	3	7	15
Reserve	11	. . .	. . .	11
Navy carriers	6	6	. . .	12

Source: William W. Kaufmann and John D. Steinbruner, *Decisions for Defense: Prospects for a New World Order* (Brookings, 1991), p. 33.

forces could be called on to counter insurgencies or narcotics activities or, as in Operation Desert Shield, to be a lead element in a major intervention, followed as needed by heavier mechanized and armored forces. On the assumption that such contingencies would require a rapid response, this command would be composed of a small but highly ready and self-sufficient force with no dependence on reserve combat formations and limited reliance on reserve support personnel, mostly volunteers with critical specialties. Six combat divisions have been marked for this command, including the Army's 82nd Airborne, 101st Air Assault, and 24th Mechanized Infantry (table 4-3). Combat support and combat service support functions, which the reserves fulfilled early in the Persian Gulf conflict, would be provided largely by the active forces for the first thirty days of a war, with reserve support units called upon as necessary as later-deploying elements of the contingency force.[99] About 40 percent of the forces supporting the contingency command would be reservists, but they would constitute only 7 percent of the support forces deployed within the first thirty days of a conflict.[100]

The Atlantic command would be assigned responsibilities for armor-heavy threats posed in Europe by one or more of the former Soviet republics or in Asia by a revitalized and perhaps even more aggressive Iraq. Reserve units would constitute eight of thirteen Army divisions,

99. Department of Defense, *Total Force Policy Report to the Congress*, December 1990, pp. 64–67.

100. General Accounting Office, *Army Force Structure: Future Reserve Roles Shaped by New Strategy, Base Force Mandates, and Gulf War* (1992), p. 23.

one of three Marine divisions, and eleven of sixteen Air Force wings allocated to this command. Of the eight reserve divisions, two would be reconstitutable cadre units, each with about 3,000 personnel, to be brought to full strength in an emergency.[101] Three of the five Army divisions designated for early reinforcement would be rounded out with a reserve brigade. The bulk of the reserve forces, in fact, would be earmarked for this command.

Finally, the Pacific command is to maintain a military presence in the western Pacific and Indian Ocean and protect American interests on the Korean peninsula. This command will be able to call on three ground divisions, five fighter wings (or their equivalents), six carrier battle groups, and a variety of other naval vessels. Planning assumes that a war against the armor-heavy North Koreans would be of medium to high intensity and last for up to 120 days. The extent to which this command would depend on reserves has not been publicly stated, but presumably it would be slight.

In sum, although the Pentagon's blueprint for the post–cold war force structure continues to rely on reserve forces, it presents a changed role for them, especially for the Army reserve. In place of the Army's twenty-eight-division force (eighteen active, ten National Guard) of the late 1980s, the base force would comprise twenty divisions: twelve active, six National Guard, and two cadre (table 4-3). One of the most conspicuous changes would be the diminished dependence on reserve units for early deployment, essentially returning them to their more traditional roles as combat reinforcements or later-deploying support forces, allowing more time for postmobilization training.

Because the prominent position it had attained under the total force policy was threatened, the National Guard quickly condemned the new strategy:

> The Base Force Strategy is built on two extremes: the reliance on a self-sufficient active Army on one end and reliance on a follow-on force developed through reconstitution over 18-24 months on the other end. Thee proposed force mix and force structure effectively ignore the cost-effective middle ground, an integrated force based on the Total Force Policy. An all active contingency force maintains full-time forces that cannot be moved within the first 60 days. Reliance on reconstitution does not meet political or economic reality.[102]

101. General Accounting Office, *Army Force Structure*, p. 31.
102. "1992 Position Statement," National Guard Association of the United States, Washington, p. 3.

The National Guard lobby was critical on other grounds as well, claiming that the strategy

> (1) would fundamentally alter the current balance between the Congress and the President in terms of entrance into and subsequent prosecution of war; (2) would deviate from the Constitutional prescription for the type and balance of military forces; (3) fails to recognize the bedrock importance of public, non-military involvement in National Defense; and (4) decreases the levels of brinkmanship or escalation available to the president.[103]

Based on these considerations, the National Guard Association and the Adjutants General Association presented an alternative calling for an Army composed of ten active divisions and ten National Guard divisions. In addition, the Guard would field six roundup or roundout brigades, a reconnaissance group, an armored cavalry regiment, and two special forces groups. The proposal also carved out forward deployment responsibilities for Guard units, including brigades based in Hawaii and Puerto Rico, an Arctic reconnaissance group in Alaska, and a crisis response mission for two Guard roundup brigades.[104] This structure would require an Army National Guard strength of 420,000 personnel (identical to the House Armed Services Committee number for fiscal year 1993), 82,000 more than planned by the administration for fiscal year 1997.

Neither the administration's nor the Guard lobby's proposals are likely to be realized because the base force concept, which underpinned the Pentagon's fiscal year 1992–97 Future Years Defense program, may have a short life. This structure was developed to fulfill the administration's promise to reduce U.S. military forces by 25 percent, a response to post–cold war calls for a "peace dividend." Although the Persian Gulf conflict delayed the reduction and raised fears that the whole plan might be premature, those concerns evaporated with the end of the war.

In fact, many critics charged that the reductions were not deep enough in light of the failed coup attempt in Moscow in August 1991, which accelerated the disintegration of the Soviet Union and rendered its military even less a threat to the West. The breakup of the Soviet Union,

103. Robert F. Ensslin, Jr., "Public Policy Dimensions of Base Force and Reconstitution Strategy for the National Guard," National Guard Association of the United States, Washington, February 1, 1992, p. i.

104. "An Alternative Force Structure Proposal," National Guard Association of the United States and Adjutants General Association of the United States, Washington, February 1992.

together with the view expressed by General Colin Powell that a second Persian Gulf conflict was unlikely, precipitated calls for reducing the previous budget agreement between the administration and Congress.[105] Amid growing signs that the base force, and especially the Atlantic command designed as a hedge against a renewed Soviet threat, would be difficult to defend, observers speculated that the Pentagon was working on "base force 2," a plan that would cut forces by 33 percent.[106]

Publicly, however, the Pentagon held fast to the base force plan with the dubious claim that the demise of the Soviet Union had already been considered in its calculations. Many observers, inside and outside the Pentagon, however, anticipated further cuts once the economic recovery became more vigorous. Smaller force structures, meanwhile, were being envisioned by critics, including Congressman Les Aspin, chairman of the House Armed Services Committee, and alternatives were presented by the Congressional Budget Office and in a congressionally mandated study led by the RAND Corporation.

Aspin contended that his analysis, unlike the administration's, responded to the dissolution of the Soviet Union rather than just the breakup of the Warsaw Pact. It resulted, he claimed, from a thorough review of force requirements rather than defense by "subtraction," and it was based on forces needed to deal with threats to important U.S. interests rather than on a more ambiguous view of what forces a superpower should have.[107]

Aspin examined four force options. Force A would be able to handle simultaneously one Iraq-sized contingency and one humanitarian relief effort. Force B would add, primarily in the form of air and naval forces, a simultaneous ability to handle a second regional contingency, especially where U.S. allies would have substantial ground forces in place; Force C would provide additionally for a rotation base to allow for a sustained Desert Storm-size deployment for an extended period. Force D would add forces sufficient to handle three simultaneous events—one Desert Storm, a regional contingency primarily involving U.S. air and naval support, and a Panama-size operation. Forces A and B would need ten Army divisions (eight active, two reserve), Force C fifteen divisions (nine active, six reserve), and Force D sixteen divisions (ten active, six re-

---

105. Wolffe, "Powell Outlines Plan."

106. *Aviation Week and Space Technology*, November 4, 1991, p. 19.

107. Les Aspin, "An Approach to Sizing American Conventional Forces in the Post-Soviet Era: Four Illustrative Options," February 25, 1992, pp. 20-21.

serve). All options included fourteen separate brigades or regiments (eight active, six reserve).[108]

Although the analysis did not contain specific recommendations, option C received the most attention once Aspin appeared to endorse it.[109] The option would give the National Guard "the significant role it wants," allowing it to be used in regional contingencies for roundout, replacement, and rotation. Four Guard brigades would be combat replacements for the first four active divisions deployed to a contingency, four brigades would round out reinforcing active divisions expected to deploy ninety days into a contingency, four Guard divisions would provide a rotation force, expected to relieve earlier deployed forces after a year's postmobilization training, and two partially manned Guard divisions would be used for reconstitution. The force C option, which allows for eight National Guard divisions and twelve separate brigades, was estimated to cost 10 percent less than the base force.[110]

A study by the Congressional Budget Office, prepared at the request of the Senate Budget Committee, presented three alternatives to the administration's 1992 proposal. In alternative one, which would increase reliance on the Army reserves, nine active, nine Guard, and two cadre divisions would replace the administration's twelve, six, and two proposal. This alternative was deemed appropriate "for a major war, which would probably occur only after substantial warning . . . or for a smaller contingency," but not for a large regional conflict.

On the assumption that it may now take years for a major threat to arise, alternative two would reduce the number of Army National Guard divisions to six and create three cadre divisions, kept in peacetime at 25 percent strength by active Army personnel and filled with reservists in wartime.

Under alternative three, Army active divisions would be reduced to six and National Guard divisions to four; eight cadre divisions, kept at 5 percent strength with active Army personnel, would be formed. This option, according to the CBO, entails greater risk but illustrates a possible approach to a reconstitution strategy.[111]

108. Aspin, "Approach to Sizing," pp. 20–21 and chart IV.

109. Les Aspin, "Toward a Meaningful Combat Role for the Army National Guard," address before the West Point Society of Washington, D.C., May 27, 1992, p. 5. Aspin's options received even more attention after he was nominated President Clinton's secretary of defense.

110. National Defense Research Institute, *Assessing Structure and Mix*, p. 173.

111. Congressional Budget Office, *Structuring U.S. Forces after the Cold War*, pp. ix–xvii.

The congressionally mandated total force study, led by the RAND Corporation, was submitted to the secretary of defense in December 1992. The study group analyzed seven Army force structures against their ability to fulfill the military requirements posed by the seven Pentagon scenarios that underlie the base force plan. In addition to the base force itself, RAND examined four additional equal-cost forces: the National Guard Association's proposal, an "enhanced" active force option, a RAND-designed alternative that would integrate the active and reserve components more fully through reforms, and a variation of this last that maintained reserve strength at the fiscal year 1993 level authorized by Congress. None of the alternatives, the study concluded, provided a sufficient hedge against the most demanding case in the Bush administration's defense planning guidance: sequential conflicts in southwest Asia and Korea.

The enhanced active force option, which would replace the base force's early reinforcement roundout divisions with full active divisions, came the closest to meeting the most demanding requirement. But because this option "would reduce reserve force levels below the Base Force and . . . the active Army manpower level that would be necessary has not been accepted by Congress," the study group concluded that "this force would be politically unacceptable."[112]

The study's preference, which maintained the fundamental structure of the base force but advocated reforms to increase reserves' participation by improving their readiness and capabilities, would use more reserve personnel than the base force but fewer than the National Guard Association's proposal. The changes advocated by the study group included the following.

—Roundout should be done at a lower organizational level (battalion or company rather than brigade) to increase the readiness and deployability of reserve units.

—The roundup concept should be used more extensively to create four-brigade divisions.

—The authorized personnel for reserve units should be increased by 8 percent.

—Active-component training units should be created specifically to provide postmobilization training.

112. National Defense Research Institute, *Assessing Structure and Mix*, pp. 165–66.

—The highly successful Air Force concept of associate units should be adopted. The concept combines active and reserve personnel in a single unit (for example, an attack helicopter unit). The reservists can train on up-to-date equipment and can give greater flexibility to the unit to conduct around-the-clock support operations.

To offset the cost of these changes, the RAND study would shift 34,000 combat support and combat service support billets from the active Army to the reserves. The application of these changes to fit the reserve strength mandated by Congress also provided the basis for another option, which was found to be no more effective than the base force configuration and less effective than the RAND-designed alternative.[113]

The study group also analyzed two options that it estimated would cost 10 percent less than the base force. The Aspin C force mix was found wanting because it would employ additional roundout brigades on the mistaken assumption that they could be fully trained in ninety days and because it failed to generate sufficient forces to meet the needs of a second contingency.[114] Finally, the application of the proposed initiatives devised by the study group to a structure equal in cost to Aspin's option C yielded a configuration that, while more effective, still failed to meet the two-contingency test.

The RAND study provided unprecedented rigor in analysis of the active-reserve mix but may be quickly overtaken by events. The base force plan and its underlying scenarios are being revised by the Clinton administration, and former Congressman Aspin's option C will probably prove too costly for Secretary of Defense Aspin.

Other proposals are sure to emerge.[115] President Clinton set about to fashion a new foreign policy and defense strategy and could discover that the two-war strategy is more than the nation can afford. In that event, the size of the reserves could be diminished further than the levels inherent in the RAND assumptions. Many matters need to be settled before consideration is given to a specific active-reserve mix of forces,

113. National Defense Research Institute, *Assessing Structure and Mix*, pp. 166, 169, 172.

114. National Defense Research Institute, *Assessing Structure and Mix*, pp. 176–77.

115. William Kaufmann, for example, has argued that the forces stipulated for the two-war contingency are larger than necessary because base force planners failed to take into account the effects of superior U.S. air power (as demonstrated during the Persian Gulf conflict) and the trade-off between air and ground forces. He has devised a structure that he contends would cost 40 percent less (in 1993 dollars) than the base force and could provide decisive victories in the Persian Gulf and in Korea. See Kaufmann, *Assessing the Base Force*, p. 83.

but if the Persian Gulf experience is any guide, rhetoric must be carefully separated from reality and missions assigned to the reserves must be based on military rather than political assessments.

The Vietnam Syndrome

Reducing reliance on reserves during the early stages of a military engagement, as proposed in the base force plan, would make it easier for a president to commit forces to combat without having to call up reserves. This flexibility would be opposed by those who support the principle, ascribed to General Creighton Abrams, of designing a force structure in such a way that the Army could not go to war without a reserve callup.

The National Guard Association, in fact, made this concern a center-piece of its opposition to the base force plan. The early involvement of citizen-soldiers, in their view, is vital to "the system of checks and balances created by the authors of the Constitution . . . based in the belief that the American people through their Congress should participate in the escalation to and subsequent prosecution of war." The report continues, "historically, the militia of citizen-soldiers [has] provided the vehicle for Congressional and public involvement in the process." Moreover, if Vietnam proved an army cannot win an unpopular war, the association asserted, in a bit of a reach, "Desert Storm proved that exercising the Constitutional process permits the army to win a war the Nation wants to fight."[116]

Conventional wisdom holds that participation by citizen-soldiers helped retain strong public approval of U.S. action in the Persian Gulf, but there is little supporting evidence. Poll data, in fact, show that 78 percent of the public supported U.S. intervention in early August 1990, but approval declined to 65 percent during the buildup as reserve call-ups were announced (figure 4-2).[117] Of course, cause and effect are difficult to sort out since so many other factors influenced American attitudes. Still, it seems reasonable to speculate that the relatively high

116. Robert F. Ensslin, Jr., "Public Policy Dimensions of Base Force and Reconstitution Strategy for the National Guard," National Guard Association, February 1, 1992, p. 1.

117. Measuring public support for U.S. involvement in the Persian Gulf crisis is not straightforward. For purposes here, a Gallup poll taken periodically between August 1990 and January 1991 is being used as the gauge. The degree of support is assumed to be the percentage of those polled who responded "Approve" to the following question: "Do you approve or disapprove of the United States' decision to send U.S. troops to Saudi Arabia as a defense against Iraq?" See *Gallup Poll Monthly*, no. 304 (January 1991), p. 11.

Figure 4-2. *Reserve Mobilizations and Public Support for the Persian Gulf Conflict, August 1990–January 1991*

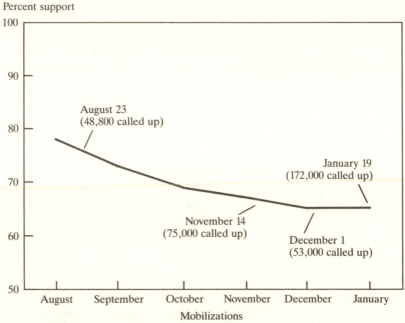

Sources: Monthly averages of polling results are in *Gallup Poll Monthly*, no. 304 (January 1991), p. 11. Size and dates of reserve mobilizations are in Robert L. Goldrich, *Persian Gulf War: U.S. Reserve Callup and Reliance on the Reserves* (Congressional Research Service, March 7, 1991), p. 3.

but gradually eroding support would have diminished much more had the conflict become protracted and bloodier. In that event the involvement of citizen-soldiers would have reinforced the deterioration of support and perhaps forced a reassessment of U.S. policy.

Nonetheless, the idea that involving reserves acts as a brake remains relevant, especially in light of the views expressed by Secretary of Defense Aspin, when as chairman of the House Armed Services Committee, he stated, "In some contingencies . . . the decision to go to war and risk large numbers of American lives must be shared with, and supported by, the American people and Congress. [former General Creighton] Abrams and [former Secretary of Defense Melvin] Laird set us on the right path for dealing with this issue, by insisting that it involve a decision to send America's citizen soldiers into war."[118] The political importance of early

118. Quoted in National Defense Research Institute, *Assessing Structure and Mix*, pp. 94–95.

combat participation by reserves was emphasized in the RAND analysis, which considered it along with cost effectiveness as a valid criterion for structuring forces. But in the absence of objective evidence, the study concluded, the belief by congressional leaders or senior policymakers that "the close integration of the reserve with active forces serves an important function . . . is *politically* sufficient to shape the alternative structures developed in this study."[119]

The Economic Rationale

That reserve units cost less than active units has contributed to the growing dependence on reserves and underpinned the contentions of advocates that the reserves constitute a national security bargain. Fielding a reserve unit in peacetime is cheaper than fielding a similar active unit. First, reservists are part-time; they command, on average, one-sixth the pay of active troops. Second, benefits and personnel replacement costs are lower. And third, because reserve units train less than active units, they incur smaller expenses for fuel, spare parts, ammunition, food, and the like.

Cost savings, however, vary widely depending on the mission (whether it is personnel or equipment intensive) and on the ratio of full-time to part-time personnel in the unit. For example, equipment-intensive Air Force and Navy reserve components incur higher operating costs than Army units. Air Force and Navy units are also staffed with larger proportions of full-time people (active-duty personnel, full-time reservists, and civilian technicians), resulting in higher personnel costs. Thus Army Reserve components cost about 25 percent of their active counterparts. Air Force Reserve units, which maintain a large cadre of full-time personnel and bear heavy equipment expenses, cost 60 to 80 percent as much as a similar active unit. The cost of operating ships in the Naval Reserve, whose companies are composed of about two-thirds active and one-third reservists, run 80 to 90 percent of a similar active naval vessel.

It has been established that unit readiness depends to a large degree on the percentage of full-time personnel, lending credence to the dictum "You get what you pay for." The readiness and performance of Air Force reserve units, for example, have consistently been respected and have become the standard for all reserve components. Accordingly, it has been

119. National Defense Research Institute, *Assessing Structure and Mix*, pp. 96–97.

suggested that the Army National Guard and Reserve should add more full-time personnel. This has been an ongoing controversy, however, because the reserve components, especially the National Guard, have resisted proposals that active Army personnel be assigned to their units, especially in higher-ranking positions.

Although an increase in full-time personnel would undoubtedly improve the readiness of Army Reserve units, it remains unclear whether the improvement would be worth the cost. The readiness of Army ground units is limited by their mission, which precludes realistic training in the available time. Air Force Reserve flying units, which are often located with similar active units, can use their built-in mobility to get to distant training facilities, if necessary, to keep their flying, gunnery, and dogfighting skills honed. The training of Army combat units, regardless of the size of their full-time component, is generally hindered by the limited availability of nearby areas for exercises necessary to simulate land combat activity.

Bureaucratic Politics

Rivalries have always existed between the active and reserve components, especially within the Army. One traditional obstacle to developing a credible reserve, according to a former reserve official, was "ingrained attitudes—the 'we versus they' approach—the declination of responsibility for Guard/Reserve problems—the view that any move to upgrade reserves would downgrade Active Forces."[120] With memories of Vietnam still vivid, the gulf between the two camps was slow to narrow during the early years of the total force policy. Many reservists believed they had not been fully accepted as members of the first team. One reserve battalion commander concluded in 1978 that professional soldiers "of high rank and position" are "throwbacks to the days of World War II and the Korean Conflict . . . [clinging] tenaciously to the shibboleth that Reserve units and personnel are totally incompetent."[121]

120. Statement of Dr. Theodore C. Marrs, deputy assistant secretary of defense for reserve affairs, in *Fiscal Year 1973 Authorization for Military Procurement, Research and Development, Construction Authorization for the Safeguard ABM, and Active Duty and Selected Reserve Strengths*, Hearings before the Senate Committee on Armed Services, 92 Cong. 2 sess. (GPO, 1972), pt. 3, p. 1625.
121. Harlon C. Herner, "A Battalion Commander Looks at Affiliation," *Military Review*, vol. 58 (October 1978), p. 42.

These rivalries tend to subside when defense budgets are increasing. It was not surprising, then, that relations seemed to improve during the early Reagan years when there was enough money to go around. The attitude of active Army officers was described by one authority on bureaucratic politics as "skeptical and concerned, but no longer condescending and contemptuous."[122]

In the second half of the decade, however, as defense spending decreased and the Army seemed to lean more and more on its reserve components, concerns among active Army officers began appearing in military journals. According to one soldier-scholar, "although publicly the Army leadership is unswerving in supporting what it calls the One Army concept, privately many officers express reservations about the ability of the reserves to fight on short notice."[123] In one of the most devastating critiques, an active Army general concluded in 1986 that "our service is literally choking on our Reserve Components." The reserves, he contended, "are not combat ready, particularly National Guard combat units. Roundout is not working. These forces will not be prepared to go to war in synchronization with their affiliated active duty formations."[124]

Other Army leaders, meanwhile, supported the reserve. Typical were the comments of the Army vice chief of staff, who boasted that the Army National Guard was at its highest readiness level in history (which probably was accurate) and had "demonstrated conclusively to our friends and potential enemies its deployability" (which probably was not).[125]

As poor as the relations between the regular and reserve leadership might have seemed, they became worse during the Persian Gulf crisis. The Pentagon leadership was careful, at least at the outset, to avoid criticism of reserve readiness. The National Guard Association and many avid supporters of the reserves on Capitol Hill were, however, vocal critics of the active military for the delay in mobilizing roundout brigades and,

122. Letter to the author from Lieutenant Colonel Wallace Earl Walker, Department of Social Sciences, U.S. Military Academy, West Point, New York, January 29, 1988.

123. A. J. Bacevich, "Old Myths: Renewing American Military Thought," *Parameters*, vol. 18 (March 1988), p. 25, note 9.

124. Letter from Major General Robert E. Wagner, commander, U.S. Army ROTC Cadet Command, to General Carl E. Vuono, commander, U.S. Army Training and Doctrine Command, August 25, 1986.

125. General Maxwell Thurman, quoted in Larry Carney, "Reserve Update 'On Track,' Thurman Says," *Army Times*, October 27, 1986, p. 20.

subsequently, for the decision to require a protracted period of training before certification of combat readiness.

Such confrontations were to be expected, especially between the Army and the National Guard Association, but the open division between the active Army and its National Guard component was not. In its "after action" report, for example, the Army National Guard did little to hide its bitterness:

> All of the Roundout Brigades and Battalions met the readiness deploya-bility criteria established by the Army Mobilization and Operations Plan-ning System (AMOPS) on the first day of federalization. The deployment readiness requirements were significantly increased for the Roundout units after they were federalized. . . . A significant number of active units did not meet AMOPS criteria before they deployed but their readiness ratings were subjectively upgraded to meet deployment requirements.[126]

Subsequent congressional action to protect the reserve components against the administration's personnel reduction plans did little to mend the rift. If anything, the Pentagon's leadership believed it was being force-fed a capability it did not want, which soured even further relations between the Army's active and reserve components.

Domestic Politics

Congressional favoritism toward the reserve forces derives from a well-organized lobby and grass-roots support generated by a network of re-serve units that has been described as an "intricate and subtle political chain that laces the country, running through village council rooms, county courthouses, and state capitals to Congress and the White House."[127] It is no coincidence, for example, that the total force concept was so warmly embraced by Congress in the early 1970s, when 108 leg-islators were not only members of reserve components but prominent on the major committees dealing with reserve legislation.[128]

126. National Guard Bureau, "Army National Guard after Action Report: Operation Desert Shield/Desert Storm," June 28, 1991, p. 7.

127. Martha Derthick, "Militia Lobby in the Missile Age—The Politics of the National Guard," in Samuel P. Huntington, ed., *Changing Patterns of Military Politics* (Crowell-Collier, 1962), p. 192.

128. Seven of fifteen members of the Senate Armed Services Committee and twelve of forty-three of the House Armed Services Committee, for example, had a reserve affiliation. For further discussion of this situation and the conflict-of-interest litigation it prompted, see Binkin, *U.S. Reserve Forces*, pp. 25–26.

This direct influence has diminished as the senators and congressmen with World War II experience have been replaced by a younger generation less likely to have served in the military, much less to maintain a reserve affiliation.

But although today's influence may be more subtle, it is no less powerful as fifty states pressure members of Congress through adjutants general, governors, and the energetic and vocal National Guard Association. Their efforts were rewarded in the late 1980s with the formation of the Senate National Guard caucus. Cochaired by Senator Wendell Ford of Kentucky, a former governor and member of the Kentucky National Guard, and Christopher Bond of Missouri, also a former governor, the organization listed sixty-nine members as of February 1992, almost equally split between Democrats and Republicans.[129]

Although the caucus did not get involved in the roundout controversy during the Persian Gulf conflict (perhaps because many of its members opposed U.S. involvement), it unanimously endorsed resisting reductions in the size and role of the Army National Guard. In May 1991, for example, fifty-four members urged Defense Secretary Richard Cheney to "rethink the cuts that have been proposed in our reserve forces," citing both the cost effectiveness of the reserves and the need to sustain the checks and balances traditionally provided by the concept of a militia.[130] In April 1992 the caucus urged Senator Sam Nunn, chairman of the Senate Armed Services Committee, to maintain for fiscal year 1993 the strengths authorized for the reserve components by Congress in the 1992 Defense Authorization Act.[131]

The federal reserve components, while not enjoying the powerful state affiliation, are beneficiaries of the National Guard's influence and, in their own right, are represented on Capitol Hill by the Reserve Officers Association.[132] Congress is receptive to the needs of the reserve com-

129. Author interview with legislative assistant to a senior member of the Senate National Guard caucus, February 1992.

130. Letter from members of the Senate National Guard Caucus to Richard B. Cheney, May 7, 1991.

131. Letter from the Senate National Guard Caucus to Sam Nunn, April 8, 1992. Senator Nunn also received an appeal from the House's forty-five-member Northeast-Midwest Congressional Coalition to resist the reductions. They were concerned that the eighteen states in their coalition which were home to 35 percent of the Army National Guard, would absorb 64 percent of the proposed reduction. Rick Maze, "Coalition Lobbies to Spare Reserves," *Army Times*, July 15, 1991, p. 7.

132. For detailed historical analyses of political influence and the Army's reserve components, see Martha Derthick, *The National Guard in Politics* (Harvard University Press,

ponents, according to a former head of the ROA, because there is "an armory or Reserve Training Center in every Congressional district, and that means there is money to be spent on men and equipment, fuel, and supplies in that district."[133] The potential economic impact of reductions in reserve units would be more localized than reductions in active personnel.

The pork barrel character of maintaining reserve strength has long frustrated presidential administrations. After Congress thwarted efforts by the Johnson administration to streamline reserve components in the 1960s, a White House staff member observed that "eco-political involvements are nowhere more clearly visible than in the status of the National Guard and Reserve programs. . . . These citizen soldiers are so solidly entrenched politically that no one in Washington dares challenge them frontally."[134] Three decades later, Defense Secretary Richard Cheney expressed similar exasperation: "If I have to keep all the Guard and reserve force structure that we currently have, I will have to spend $20 billion over the next five years on force structure that no longer has a mission."[135] Another observer said, "If the Defense Department fails to make a strong case for following its force-cutting plan, the congressional solution may be 'politics as usual.' . . . In that case, the reserves may be shaped more by their voting strength than for their military utility."[136]

The Fundamental Issues

Designing a structure for U.S. military forces, particularly defining the role of the Army's reserve components, presents a formidable challenge, given the clamor of competing demands. My intention is not to prescribe a specific mix of Army active and reserve forces—that involves relating U.S. foreign policy to national security strategy and requires

1965); and William F. Levantrosser, *Congress and the Citizen-Soldier: Legislative Policymaking for the Federal Armed Forces Reserve* (Ohio State University Press, 1967).

133. Robert H. Spiro, Jr., quoted in Michael Ganley, "Who's Guarding the Guard and Reserve?" *Armed Forces Journal International* (May 1986), p. 66. These armories and training centers are also a focus of community social life in many small towns.

134. Douglass Cater, *Power in Washington: A Critical Look at Today's Struggle to Govern in the Nation's Capital* (Random House, 1964), p. 41.

135. Rowan Scarborough, "Cheney Drops Guard, Gets Hit," *Washington Times*, November 11, 1991, p. 1.

136. William Matthews, "Total War: Active, Reserve Forces Fight for Defense Dollars," *Army Times*, April 20, 1992, p. 14.

assessments of military threats, the simultaneity of those threats, and assumptions about warning time, among other considerations. These matters need to be settled through debate and negotiations between the administration and Congress. Nevertheless, there are fundamental questions that need to be resolved before the detailed business of devising any combination of active and reserve forces is addressed.

—What state of readiness can reserve units be expected to maintain, how much postmobilization training would they need, how soon could they be deployed, and how well would they perform their assigned missions?

—Is the "Abrams Doctrine"—structuring the Army so it cannot go to war without the reserves—an appropriate hedge against U.S. involvement in an unpopular war?

—Is limited presidential authority to mobilize troops a wise policy?

—What implications should the National Guard's responsibilities in the states hold for the design of the total Army?

—Is it realistic to assume that active Army personnel and their reserve counterparts can work in harmony, given the ever widening schism between them?

—What means are available to limit the influence of domestic politics on the design of force structure?

Capabilities, Limitations, and Appropriate Roles

The various assessments of the Army's reserve components during the Persian Gulf conflict present conflicting views of their readiness and post-mobilization training. They offer anecdotes about the performance of the units but virtually no analysis. Considering the exaggerations inherent in the parochial rhetoric of the active Army and its reserve components on the one hand, and the atypical nature of the Gulf conflict on the other, one should exercise caution in drawing lessons from the experience.

One of the few conclusions to have achieved a consensus is that Army reserve units with noncombat missions can sustain a higher level of readiness for deployment than combat units can. Although supporters of the Army National Guard would take exception, the active Army's assessment that a combat brigade would require a minimum of ninety days' training before deployment (the Guard says forty-five to sixty days) and a combat division a full year (the Guard says six months) was accepted generally, most importantly by Congressman (and now Secretary of Defense) Aspin, who concluded, "If we're going to make a mistake, let's do it on the side of safety . . . we should adopt the active Army's conservative planning factors for post-mobilization training."[137] The RAND study, however, concluded that it would be prudent to allow 128 days for a brigade to attain the appropriate level of combat readiness.[138]

These estimates bring into question the legitimacy of the Pentagon's cold war contingency planning, which called for the deployment of National Guard combat units to the European theater much earlier than is now considered feasible. The assignment of roundout brigades to divisions with rapid deployment responsibilities is especially suspect. Also questionable is the credibility of earmarking National Guard brigades for crisis response or early reinforcement, as envisioned in the plan advanced by the National Guard Association. All this suggests that the Guard's role assigned in the base force plan would be less a gamble.[139]

Moreover, to the extent the Pentagon planners' assumptions are realistic, none of the military campaigns for the seven scenarios they devised, apart from a possible protracted confrontation with some resurgent global power, will last long enough for the reserve combat units to participate significantly. And although maintaining a combat capability as a hedge against a longer war may appear reasonable, the Pentagon's assumption of substantial advance warning suggests that there would be enough time to reconstitute combat divisions. The strongest counterarguments would be, first, that Pentagon planning aside, it is still prudent to hedge against unforeseen contingencies, and second, that as long as the National Guard exists to fulfill state responsibilities, its capabilities might as well be exploited for federal missions.

Unlike reserve combat units, reserve support units generally lived up to expectations of their readiness. According to the Army, performance in Desert Shield indicated that combat support and combat service support units could be made ready for deployment thirty to forty-five days after mobilization. Based on the evidence, the Army's dependence on its reserve components for much of its support was a cost-effective policy worthy of continuation. Its proposal to minimize the use of reserve support units in early deployment, as indicated in the base force plan, ap-

---

137. Aspin, "Toward a Meaningful Combat Role," p. 3.

138. National Defense Research Institute, *Assessing Structure and Mix*, p. xxvii.

139. The exception would be if there was sufficient warning time before the outbreak of hostilities to ready the National Guard units. Apparently the base force plan assumes that future conflicts will come as bolts out of the blue rather than after protracted diplomatic discussions.

pears to stem from bureaucratic politics as much as technical considerations and should be reconsidered. The support skills needed principally in wartime, such as expertise with languages and skills with water purification techniques, should be maintained in the reserves. For a wide range of contingencies, it would appear practical to assign military police, transportation, supply, and other combat service support functions to reserve units.

Hedging against Unpopular Wars

A principal rationale for heavy and early reliance on reserve forces is that the involvement of citizen-soldiers would prevent presidents from sliding into major military commitments without obtaining public consensus. Many supporters of the reserves believe this brake on presidential powers remains necessary.[140]

Although it has been argued that the popular support for the Persian Gulf conflict demonstrated that the Abrams doctrine worked, there is little evidence connecting that support to the participation by reservists or suggesting that a national debate was prompted by their call-up. In fact, President Bush called up thousands of reservists before any public discussion or congressional consultations took place. And when he proclaimed, without a clear vision of the ultimate military consequences, that Iraq's aggression "would not stand," he had no way of knowing whether he was getting the nation involved in what might become an unpopular military venture. The president was betting that public and congressional support would follow.[141]

140. In fact, however, legislation in 1976 granted the president authority to call up 50,000 reservists without declaring the national emergency that would have promoted public debate. The argument was further compromised when Congress twice expanded the authority, raising the number to 200,000.

141. This decision violated one of the six criteria for U.S. involvement in military actions that had been established by Secretary of Defense Caspar Weinberger in 1984 to ensure that the United States would not drift into another Vietnam. "Before the U.S. commits combat forces abroad," he said, "there must be some reasonable assurance we will have the support of the American people and their elected representatives in Congress. We cannot fight a battle with the Congress at home while asking our troops to win a war overseas or, as in the case of Vietnam, in effect asking our troops not to win but just to be there." For a discussion of the criteria, see Richard Halloran, "U.S. Will Not Drift into a Latin War, Weinberger Says," *New York Times*, November 29, 1984, p. A1.

Just what Weinberger meant by "reasonable assurance" is unclear. Arguably, the conditions surrounding the Persian Gulf conflict did not provide ample time for President Bush

It is difficult to conclude, therefore, that the Army's reliance on the reserves influenced the president's decision, at least at the outset of the crisis. To give any credence to the Abrams doctrine, one would have to speculate that if the strategy backfired in some way or had the military campaign bogged down, participation by reservists would have promoted an earlier public debate.

Even if the concept of the brake on presidential haste had worked, is the principle, which has largely escaped public scrutiny, in the national interest? Such strictures, by virtually requiring a referendum before force is employed, may hamper too much the flexibility of the president to use military force as an instrument of foreign policy. This matter, of course, is at the heart of the enduring debate over warmaking authority, as evidenced in the controversy over the validity of the War Powers Act, which presidents have ignored and Congress appears unwilling to test. Still, the nation is probably better served if decisions about war are handled through the legislative process rather than compelled through force structure design.

Call-up Authority

President Bush's decision to federalize reservists for the Persian Gulf conflict under the limited call-up authority that has been on the books since 1976 also caused controversy. Although it seemed to make good sense when the extent of the military buildup was uncertain, the president's reliance on the provision for five months into the crisis hamstrung the Army. Restrictions on the number and type of reservists who could be called and on the duration of their service created inefficiencies in filling support requirements and discouraged calling up units that would have needed prolonged postmobilization training.

Those who favor the flexibility that the limited authority affords the president would solve the problem by doubling the time—from six months to one year—that reservists could serve under its provisions. Alternatively, the limited authority, already expanded well beyond the original legislation, may provide the president too much leeway.

---

to conduct a national referendum or to marshal consensus in a Congress with which he was strongly at odds. It is also interesting to note that, if the tests are literally interpreted, Weinberger probably violated his own criteria when he committed U.S. forces in 1987 to protect oil tankers in the Persian Gulf.

The initial legislation, with a ceiling of 50,000, was intended to give the chief executive the flexibility to *begin* preparations for mobilization during an international crisis without unduly heightening tensions. But Congress doubled the ceiling twice, providing the president an unprecedented a degree of discretionary authority that may invite the creeping involvement in military operations that the Pentagon and Congress especially wanted to avoid. President Bush, for example, was still mobilizing reservists under the limited authority in November 1990 when he decided to double the size of the deployment to prepare for offensive operations—a situation that should have triggered the use of the broader authority.

As a result, the distinction between the conditions under which limited or broader authorities are appropriate has become blurred, and Congress should reconsider the legislation in this light. At a minimum, it should reimpose the original ceiling of 50,000 to ensure the authority is used only as an initial step in a potential conflict. On the premise that reserve forces will be less important in future contingencies, a president would not need emergency authority to call up more than 50,000 reservists *before* declaring a national emergency and exercising partial mobilization authority. Those who continue to subscribe to the Abrams doctrine would probably favor an even lower ceiling for the limited authority in order to promote an earlier national debate.

The Guard's State Role

Proposals to reduce the size of the National Guard have been met with charges that reductions would cripple the guard's abilities to fulfill its domestic missions. The National Guard, it has been pointed out, is a major participant in the war on drugs. It is also the "first line of local, state and regional response to natural disasters and civil disturbances and through its numerous community programs ranging from youth programs to role modeling for the leaders of tomorrow, it contributes to improving the moral fabric of the Nation."[142] There is little evidence, however, that reductions on the order of those proposed by the Bush administration would have a significant effect on the Guard's domestic

---

142. Ensslin, "Public Policy Dimensions," p. 5. The performance of the California National Guard during the Los Angeles riots, however, was heavily criticized in a review ordered by Governor Pete Wilson. See Daniel M. Weintraub, "Report on L.A. Riots Blasts National Guard," *Los Angeles Times*, Washington ed., December 3, 1992, p. 1.

responsibilities. Obviously, individual states would have different requirements, but the magnitude of those needs remains unclear. And if the state mission is considered important, it would seem that the Guard would be more interested in combat service support structure—military police, transportation, engineering, and construction units—that would be much more relevant than combat maneuver units for meeting exigencies imposed by such events as the Los Angeles riots and Hurricane Andrew in 1992.

Finally, even if it is unrealistic to assume that the coveted combat function could be stripped from the Guard, the type of combat units to be retained deserve further consideration. For example, motorized infantry units would be better suited for state missions, such as riot control, than would the mechanized and armored divisions now planned.

Rapprochement of the Active Army and the National Guard

Relations between the active Army and its National Guard component have never been worse. The rivalry has always been present, but rarely has the internecine warfare been waged in public. That changed with the Persian Gulf conflict when the active Army chose not to mobilize the roundout brigades and substituted active Army support commands, staffed with senior active-duty officers, for many reserve commands. Emboldened by the support of congressional champions, the National Guard lobby attacked the Army leadership with unprecedented fervor, creating a rift that will be difficult to close. Notwithstanding the repeated claims that the situation has been exaggerated, the rivalry may have become too ingrained and too emotional to be resolved anytime soon.

Cooperation cannot be legislated, but it can be hoped that both sides will recognize that harmony is preferable to conflict. However, to the extent that the durability of this rivalry may be a sign of its intractability, plans for mixing active and reserve components must take these relations into consideration.

Breaking the Logjam

Analysts have been discouraged from grappling with the mix of active and reserve Army forces because such matters have been settled by political decisions rather than technical considerations. Even Secretary of Defense Robert McNamara's whiz kids in the 1960s, whose fame was based on their aggressive challenges of the military's sacred cows, backed away from taking this bull by the horns.

The Pentagon's total force study in 1990 was assailed by Congress as emanating from an active military establishment seeking to secure its position in a zero-sum game. The congressionally mandated study done by RAND in 1992 will be better received on Capitol Hill, tilting as it does toward reserve interests, but the Army leadership, despite new civilian superiors, will probably continue lobbying to protect its domain. The Army's case, after all, is reinforced by the RAND study's finding that an active-Army-intensive force bested all other options in cost-effectiveness.

The breadth and depth of political interest in the mix of military forces is reminiscent of the interest focused on proposed base closures, which had the administration and Congress at loggerheads for so many years. The parallels are so close, in fact, that the method used to break the logjam on base closures should be considered for resolving the composition of the forces. An executive branch commission was established to provide the secretary of defense and Congress with recommendations on which installations could be closed or realigned. What made that effort successful where other commissions had failed was that the Base Closure and Realignment Act of 1988 established a process for arriving at a decision by the secretary of defense and review by Congress. Most important, it provided for the selective waiver of laws that had frustrated previous efforts to close bases.

Under the ground rules, the secretary of defense had either to accept or reject the entire package of recommendations and transmit this decision to Congress. The transmittal would trigger an expedited review, giving Congress forty-five days to consider the recommendation, which could only be overridden by a joint resolution of disapproval. The joint resolution, of course, could be vetoed, and if the veto were sustained, the closures would take effect. The hurdles in the way of anyone wishing to block the proposal contributed to the success of the venture.

A similar process could be established for deciding on a force mix. A bipartisan commission could be established to analyze the mix and make its recommendations to the secretary of defense and Congress under the same ground rules governing the closure recommendations. Admittedly, force structure decisions are far more complex than those involving base closures, but there is an ample supply of experts on all sides of the subject, both at the policymaking and analytic levels. Moreover, unlike the base closure commission, which had little research to draw on, a Total Force Commission would have access to a substantial repository of studies and analyses. Its principal challenges would be to sift through the technical, political, and bureaucratic claims, separate rhetoric from reality, and find a balance that would best meet U.S. national security interests.

CHAPTER FIVE

Who Will Fight the Next War?

THE PERSIAN GULF conflict, the first major test of the nation's all-volunteer force, resulted in a lopsided victory for the United States and its coalition partners and aroused in many Americans a depth of patriotism not witnessed since the end of World War II. The conflict left another legacy, more subtle perhaps, but also longer lasting: unsettled questions about who should fight the nation's wars.

The commitment of U.S. armed forces to potentially bloody and prolonged combat in the desert sands of the Arabian peninsula served as a wakeup call for the American public, which had been indifferent to the transformations in the makeup of the armed services that followed the adoption of an all-volunteer force in 1973. What it now saw, to its surprise, was a contemporary military in many ways far removed from any the nation had previously sent to war.

Record proportions of American women—the nation's mothers, daughters, sisters, and girlfriends—were exposed to perils from which, by long and deep tradition, they had previously been shielded. African Americans, among the most disadvantaged members of society, were disproportionately represented, especially in the ground combat forces. And the nation's citizen-soldiers, who had not participated extensively in combat since the Korean War, now figured prominently in the nation's war plans.

Public reactions were mixed. Some welcomed the cultural diversity of the armed forces, impressed that the military was such an effective engine of social reform. Others were uneasy, if not downright concerned, that a force built to fit social and political norms in peacetime would compromise military effectiveness and exact a penalty in wartime. Most people, however, appeared ambivalent. The absence of a consensus is not surprising because the composition of the armed forces involves a complicated mix of military, social, and political considerations and influences. Indeed as the analyses in the previous chapters revealed, the trade-offs are not straightforward, and there are many issues over which reasonable people will disagree.

Women as Warriors?

The deployment of record numbers of military women to the Persian Gulf was greeted with widespread interest, and among the women involved there was a conviction that they would finally be able to prove their mettle. And indeed, their experience debunked one preconception after another. Women appeared to adapt as well as men to the austere living conditions and the deprivations common to a military deployment. Contrary to some predictions, the American public appeared resigned to the fact that women as well as men could lose their lives or be taken prisoner.

The crucial issue regarding women that emerged from the conflict was not so much whether women belonged in the military but whether they should be permitted to serve in combat. Support for removing combat restrictions on them grew rapidly after the cessation of hostilities, in part because the relatively low-risk airwar followed by a remarkably brief and largely unopposed ground campaign had created the impression that hand-to-hand combat and its accompanying physical demands and emotional strains had become anachronisms as computers and stand-off weapons had replaced rifles and bayonets on the modern battlefield.

The issue of whether to allow women to engage in combat pits two powerful forces in American society—national security and equal opportunity—against one another. The choice is difficult because it requires an assessment of the tradeoff between the uncertain risk to national security of making fundamental changes in the culture of combat units, on one hand, and, on the other, furthering a social imperative that, in the end, would probably benefit only a limited number of women.

Where the risks to national security appear few, as with combat aircraft units and naval combat ships, repealing the remaining laws that restrict women is justified. The arguments some have presented about women's limited physical strength and aptitude, their detrimental impact on combat unit effectiveness and cohesion, and their inevitable vulnerability to conscription (should it become necessary) have little relevance to the Air Force and Navy.

The argument that enormous costs would be incurred to house women also appears misplaced. The armed forces have already demonstrated they can provide living accommodations for large numbers of women without incurring unreasonable costs. Modifications to provide coed facilities in the confines of ships, probably the most challenging test, have been accomplished with few difficulties. Retrofitting weapon systems to accommodate a greater proportion of women, however, would be a more costly proposition and unworthy of consideration unless women could be expected to constitute a reasonable proportion of those operating the systems. In the more likely event that few women would be assigned to combat units, it would be more efficient to accept only those whose anthropometric characteristics matched current equipment design.

How many women the Air Force and Navy would assign to combat duties, however, is an open question. If history is any guide, too much should not be expected. It is likely, moreover, that in the face of substantial force reductions and corresponding decreases in the number of pilot training slots and seagoing billets, few women will be involved. Furthermore, although the percentage of women who might be interested in filling combat positions remains uncertain, by most indications it is not large. Under the circumstances, it is unlikely that women will constitute more than a small percentage of combat fighter pilots or combat ship personnel. The services would therefore be wise to design programs to avoid the types of problems that tokenism has caused in the past.

In the case of ground combat, however, the evidence provides valid reasons for restricting women from serving in Army and Marine Corps infantry or armor units, or in the Army Rangers, Navy SEALS, or other special forces units. Although some of the arguments for keeping women out can be discounted as old chestnuts, others should not be summarily dismissed.

Among the most common rationales for excluding women from ground combat has been their lack of the necessary physical or emotional attributes. But despite all the experience in all the wars the nation has been involved in, there is little scientific evidence linking physical or emotional attributes to ground combat performance. Some women would be at least as capable, by any measure, as the marginally qualified male combat infantryman or armor crewman.

Also, concerns that the nation was not prepared to accept women being killed on the battlefield or taken prisoner were not realized during the Persian Gulf conflict. Instead, the distinctions between combat and noncombat have narrowed with changes in the tactics and weapons of war and have reinforced the argument that the hazards of war are not confined to combat personnel. There was little to indicate, moreover, that the public was especially sensitive to the gender implications of casualty and prisoner-of-war statistics.

The concerns relating to the possible damaging effect women would have on combat unit cohesion are the most difficult to dismiss. There is little empirical basis for predicting how the presence of women would affect the combat performance of men because women have not routinely been a part of combat activities in any nation's military. But the link between male bonding and ground combat performance is strongly rooted in tradition. Placing the burden of proof on the few advocates who support ground combat roles for women to demonstrate that unit effectiveness would not be diminished—something virtually impossible to do without observing women in those roles—may appear to be a catch-22 situation, but it was one that even the disparate factions of the Presidential Commission on the Assignment of Women in the Armed Forces unanimously agreed upon.

The Black Dilemma

As some women fight for the right to fight, there is a concurrent question of whether African Americans, who successfully waged a similar battle decades ago, have carried the quest too far. The dramatic growth in blacks' participation in the nation's armed forces, especially in the Army, since the end of the draft has provided many African Americans with economic and social opportunities they were unable to find in the civilian world. At the same time, however, their participation has meant that they could suffer more than their fair share of casualties in wartime. This dilemma of benefits versus burdens had gone largely unnoticed until the Persian Gulf conflict.

Before the conflict, the public seemed unconcerned with blacks' participation in the military. Among black leaders, the few who criticized the potential inequities were outnumbered by those who applauded the military as a model for equal opportunity. Most, however, remained silent. The ambivalence stemmed from the quandary posed by perceptions of equity, which are greatly influenced by the perceived ratio of benefits to burdens. When the benefits of military service outweigh the burdens, as they do in peacetime, the overrepresentation of blacks is considered a contribution to true social equity. When the burdens outweigh the benefits, as they may in wartime, overrepresentation is perceived as systemic inequity.

Predictably, this phenomenon occurred in conjunction with the Persian Gulf conflict when, spearheaded by a small group of African-American leaders warning of an inequitable distribution of casualties, black support for U.S. involvement was far weaker than overall public support. The nation was fortunate: the gloomy casualty predictions failed to materialize. In fact, blacks accounted for 17 percent of the deaths, a proportion much less than their representation in combat.

It is not a far reach, however, to speculate that had the conflict unfolded according to most predictions, more casualties among ground forces would have occurred and blacks would have suffered a larger proportion of them. The criticism of the African American leaders would have intensified, and the nation could have experienced serious racial discord at a critical juncture. The questions are, then, should the nation attempt to hedge against the divisive effects of disproportionate black casualties in future military conflicts and, if so, how?

The analysis in chapter 3 concludes that fielding a military force, especially an army, that roughly reflects the racial and ethnic makeup of American society is a worthy objective but one that appears unattainable in the short run. The few options available for achieving such a reflection would require interventionary policies, such as the application of quotas, that would fail tests of social equity or political correctness. Over the longer term, as America comes to grips with its underlying social and educational problems, the status of African Americans will improve, their employment prospects will brighten, and their propensities for military service will come closer to matching those of whites.

Until then, if U.S. troops get involved in another major ground conflict, the nation may again have to confront racial divisiveness at a time when it could least afford to do so. One would hope, as a result of the Persian Gulf experience, the American public has a better understanding of the dilemma and a greater sense of urgency for initiating programs to reverse the decades of social and educational neglect responsible for creating it.

The Role of Weekend Warriors

The Persian Gulf conflict, the first test of the Pentagon's total force policy, necessitated the largest call-up of reservists since the Korean War. The citizen-soldiers won widespread plaudits in recognition of their sacrifices when, on short notice, they were uprooted from their families and civilian occupations to serve the nation. The notable successes during the conflict, however, were overshadowed by the internecine war that erupted between the Army and its National Guard component over the Army's failure to deploy several National Guard roundout brigades, which were the centerpieces of the total force policy. The National Guard and its congressional supporters believed that the Army, largely out of a parochial sense of Guard inferiority, had denied the National Guard an opportunity to showcase its premier units. Controversies were ignited over reserves' state of readiness, possible Army double standards, and in the end, the soundness of the roundout concept itself.

A great deal was at stake because a reexamination of the role of reserve forces in general and the Army National Guard combat units in particular became especially important with the end of the cold war. Considering revised military planning assumptions and widely accepted views about the capabilities of reserve combat formations, chapter 4 suggested it would be imprudent to earmark National Guard combat brigades for crisis response or for early reinforcement missions. At the same time, however, certain reserve combat support and service support units, whose capabilities were demonstrated during the Persian Gulf conflict, warrant wider and earlier use than is envisioned in Pentagon contingency planning.

Forging agreement over the appropriate role for the reserve forces will be difficult, however, because in matters relating to the reserves, military considerations tend to be eclipsed by domestic politics and bureaucratic rivalries. Inasmuch as the normal force planning and legislative processes are unlikely to resolve this matter on its technical merits, establishing a blue-ribbon commission similar to the one that broke the political logjam over closing military bases should be considered.

The future of American fighting forces will hinge on how these questions are resolved. The nation needs to better understand the composition of its fighting forces, to assess its attitudes toward who will fight its wars, and to examine the options available for influencing the social distribution of peril. The time for public involvement is now, while the memories of the Persian Gulf conflict are still reasonably fresh and while a fundamental rethinking of the post–cold war military establishment is under way.

Index

Abrams, Gen. Creighton W., 110, 149, 150
Abzug, Bella S., 46n
Adelsberger, Bernard, 22n, 94n
African Americans in armed forces, 2–3;
appeal of military, 72–73, 89–90;
benefits-burden dilemma, 74–76;
discriminatory racial policies, 64–65,
67–68, 73–74; entrance test and, 92, 95–
99; historical background, 62–70;
integration of armed forces, 66–67; job
opportunities protection, 94–99;
occupations, 78, 80; as proportion of
total armed forces, 1, 61; prospects,
100–01; quotas, 94; racial incidents, 70;
segregated regiments, 63–64; studies on,
66, 67, 69, 70–71. *See also* Racial
imbalance in armed forces
Air combat, unit cohesion and, 40n
Air Force: African Americans admitted,
65; costs of gender integration, 54, 56–
57; functional capacity standard, 29;
pregnancy policy, 13–14; racial
integration, 67; women, numbers, 9;
women in combat issue, 11–12, 45
Air Force Academy, 42
Air Force Reserve, 108, 117, 119, 151, 152
Air National Guard, 108
Albro, Ames S., Jr., 5n
Alexander, Clifford L., Jr., 75, 94
Allen, William E., 98n
Ambrose, Stephen E., 64n, 65n, 66n
Armed Forces Qualification Test (AFQT),
90n
Armed Services Vocational Aptitude
Battery (ASVAB). *See* Entrance test of
armed forces
Army: functional capacity standard, 29,
30; male recruits, problems regarding,
8, 9. *See also* African Americans in

armed forces; Combat role for women;
Racial imbalance in armed forces;
Women in armed forces
Army Board to Study the Utilization of
Negro Manpower (Chamberlin board),
66
Army National Guard. *See* Reserve forces
Army Reserve. *See* Reserve forces
Aspin, Les, 84n, 120n, 123n, 124, 130n,
145–46, 148, 150, 157–58
Atlantic command, 142–43

Bacevich, A. J., 153n
Bach, Shirley J., 4n, 6n
Bagley, Adm. Worth, 41n
Bailey, Brig. Gen. Mildred C., 14
Barber, James A., Jr., 64n
Barkalow, Capt. Carol, 21n
Base Closure and Realignment Act of
1988, 163
Base force plan, 116, 133, 137; allocation
of forces, 142; alternative proposals,
143–44, 145–49; Atlantic forces, 142–43;
bureaucratic politics and, 152–54;
combat role for reserve forces, 139;
contingency (rapid deployment) forces,
141–42; domestic politics and, 154–56;
economic rationale, 151–52; force
structure considerations, 139–49;
inclination of government to use military
and, 149–51; Pacific forces, 143;
readiness considerations, 137–39;
reductions in force levels, 144–45; U.S.
military involvement and, 140–41
Becraft, Carolyn, 12n, 13n, 15, 30n, 34,
44n
Berlin crisis of *1961,* 104–5
Binder, David, 94n

173